BURNLEY FC
HISTORY QUIZ

ANSWERS AND
FACTS

Mike Prosser

Burnley FC History Quiz Answers and Facts

This book was first published in Great Britain in paperback during October 2022.

The moral right of Mike Prosser is to be identified as the author of this work, in accordance with the Copyright, Designs and Patents Act of 1988.

Email: ads2life@btinternet.com

ISBN: 979-8358687172

This publication is dedicated to my best friend and Burnley FC supporter

Peter Clarke who sadly passed away in Malta in November 2021.

He was a true Clarets fan and will be remembered by all including the two Burnley footballing legends who are forwording this book.

Foreword from Colin Waldron. Prepared by Paul Fletcher MBE

I'm always pleased to be asked to write a foreword for a new book about Burnley FC, as after I started my career as a forward at Bury FC until some bright spark on the coaching side decided I would make a better defender than a forward- and my glory days scoring goals effectively ended then. My forewords forever - only on paper.

My association and love-affair with Burnley Football Club began on that day and still goes on today as I now got over the run-ins I had with Chairman Bob Lord and Harry Potts and the sadness with Jimmy Adamson after he sold me to Manchester United. I forgave him a couple of years later when he signed me up for Sunderland where I played for a couple of years until I joined the football -train to America, when, like many other English players we tried to establish the beautiful game across the pond.

It's been wonderful to see my Club yo-yo in and out of the Premiership over the Sean Dyche reign, we all knew that our town club (with a capacity of 21,000 fans) could never establish itself in the biggest league in world football amidst the City Clubs of the Manchester United's , the Chelsea's, the Arsenals, and even Newcastle United who bought their way out of relegation by strengthening their team with Burnley players- after they'd appointed our ex manager earlier in the 2021-22 season.

This nicely leads me on to the curious questions and facts that Mike has cleverly assembled together in this fascinating book, I've always been a fan of 'questions and answers' especially when it's about my old club and the teams that it represented. I'm sure my name and the names of Adamson's wonderful Team of the 70's will be amongst these questions somewhere and the answers will bring back many memories for us all to feel proud about.

One strange fact about Burnley FC is that a number of its players (me included), now in their 70's who arrived at the Club as young players, married Burnley girls, then stayed in the area once their careers were over, still meet up on a regular basis for either coffee in the Burnley Costa on Friday mornings or drinks in a Burnley pub on Thursday evenings. I don't know any other Club in the land where this happens.

Colin Waldron, Burnley FC Captain 1968-69 and 1973-76
356 senior appearances for Burnley October 1967 to June 1976

Paul Fletcher MBE, Burnley player March 1971 to February 1980
349(3) senior appearances. 86 goals scored.

Preface

Having supported Burnley for many years, I have always been intrigued with the history of the Club and have in the past written three books mostly on that subject.

I have been involved with the London Supporters bi Monthly magazine "To Write Home About" and have prepared a 10 question multi choice History Quiz for the past eleven years with thanks to editor Phil Whalley and its fellow members.

My thoughts were to do a History Quiz book with a difference with the answers at the back of the book which also explains the facts to the answers. I have prepared this as accurately as possible and it also gives an insight to the many younger fan base that are now supporting this great Football Club.

I would also like to thank the support I have had in the past from the London Clarets and Burnley supporter Brian Speak and others.

Thanks also go out to ex Burnley legends Colin Waldron and Paul Fletcher MBE for forewording this publication.

Quiz 1

1. How many League goals did leading league goalscorer Benny Green score in the 1909–10 season?

   A. 12.   **B.** 16.   **C.** 18.

2. Burnley's famous half back line-up of Halley, Boyle and Watson first played together in which season?

   A. 1909–10.   **B.** 1912–13.   **C.** 1913–14.

3. Who was the first Burnley player to have captained England?

   A. Louis Page.   **B.** Jack Hill.   **C.** Tommy Boyle.

4. Who was Burnley's captain in the 2008–09 Championship Play-off Final?

   A. Steven Caldwell.   **B.** Graham Alexander.   **C.** Clarke Carlisle.

5. What Nationality was 1955–56 leading league goalscorer Peter McKay?

   A. Welsh.   **B.** English.   **C.** Scottish.

6. Who was the Burnley leading League goalscorer in the 2008–09 season?

   A. Martin Paterson.   **B.** Kevin McDonald.   **C.** Robbie Blake.

7. How many full League appearances did goalkeeper Marlon Beresford make for Burnley?

   A. 240.   **B.** 265.   **C.** 286.

8   Who was Burnley's first player manager?

    A. Jimmy Mullen.   **B.** Adrian Heath.   **C.** Chris Waddle.

9. Leading league goalscorer Gareth Taylor scored how many goals in the 2001–02 season?

    A. 16.   **B.** 17.   C. 18.

10. Which manager replaced Stan Ternent at Burnley in 2004?

    A. Owen Coyle.   **B.** Brian Laws.   **C.** Stephen Cotterill.

Quiz 2

1. Who replaced Burnley manager Jimmy Adamson in January 1976?
   A. Harry Potts.   **B.** Brian Miller.   **C.** Joe Brown.

2. Who were Burnley's joint top League goalscorers with 13 goals in the 1975–76 season?
   A. Hankin and Noble.   **B.** Hankin and Flynn.   **C.** Fletcher and Hankin.

3. Who joined Burnley for a club record fee of £100,000 in 1976?
   A. Mike Summerbee.   **B.** Leighton James.   **C.** Tony Morley.

4. What was Burnley's new first choice strip for the 1975–76 season?
   A. Claret and Blue halves.   **B.** Claret and Blue quarters.
   C. Claret and Blue with a blue V on the chest.

5. Colin Waldron's last game for Burnley on 27 March 1976 was against which League club?
   A. Liverpool.   **B.** Leeds United.   **C.** Southampton

6. On 16 October 1976, Burnley played their 3.000th League game against which club?
   A. Charlton Athletic.   **B.** Orient.   **C.** Fulham.

7. Burnley were beaten in the third round of the FA Cup in January 1976 by which club?
   A. Leicester City.   **B.** Hereford United.   **C.** Blackpool.

8. How many points did Burnley have when they were relegated from the First Division in the 1975–76 season?

    A. 28.   **B.** 29.   **C.** 30.

9. To which club was Ray Hankin transferred to in September 1976?

    A. Manchester City.   **B.** Arsenal.   **C.** Leeds United.

10. Who were Burnley's first league opponents in their return to the Second Division on 21 August 1976?

    A. Fulham.   **B.** Wolverhampton Wanderers   **C.** Luton Town.

Quiz 3

1. Bert Freeman scored a total of 36 goals in the 1912–13 season. How many of these were scored in the FA Cup rounds?

   A. 4.   **B.** 5.   **C.** 6.

2. Who was Burnley's first Welsh international?
   A. Brian Flynn.   **B.** Leighton James.   **C.** Stan Bowsher.

3. When goalkeeper Colin McDonald signed for Burnley in 1950, which non-league club was he loaned out too?

   A. Cambridge United.   **B.** Headington United.   **C.** Peterborough United.

4. Who were Burnley's FA Cup semi-final opponents in 1913?
   A. Bradford City.   **B** Sunderland.   **C.** Aston Villa.

5. Leading Burnley goalscorer George Beel in his nine years at the club scored how many hat-tricks ?

   A. 7.   **B.** 8.   **C.** 11.

6. Who were Burnley's first English opponents on foreign soil?
   A. Manchester United.   **B.** Sunderland.   **C.** Liverpool.

7. Who replaced manager Tom Bromilow in 1936?
   A. Billy Dougall.   **B.** Ray Bennion.   **C.** The Burnley selection committee.

8. Burnley goalkeeper Jack Hillman was the first England keeper to concede a penalty.

   A. True.   **B.** False.

9. When brothers David and John Walders joined Burnley in the early 1900s, which club did they previously play for?

   A. Barrow.   **B.** Blackpool.   **C.** Workington.

10. Gillingham's forward Bob Taylor scored all 5 goals in Burnley's 0–5 defeat in February 1999 at Turf Moor?

    A. True.   **B** False.

Quiz 4

1. With the record purchase from Brentford of Andre Gray in August 2015, who was the previous purchase from the London side?

   A. William Green 1903.   **B.** Charlie Fletcher. 1936.   **C.** Kevin Ball 2000.

2. Who were Burnley's first opponents outside of Lancashire in 1885?

   A. Burslem Port Vale.   **B.** West Bromwich Albion.   **C.** Walsall Town.

3. Who were Burnley's first Scottish opponents at Turf Moor in 1885?

   A. Kilmarnock.   **B.** Glasgow Northern.   **C.** Cowlairs.

4. Who was Burnley's first Scottish international player?

   A. Willie Morgan.   **B.** Adam Blacklaw.   **C.** John Aird.

5. Who were runners up to Burnley in the Division Four Championship season?

   A. Mansfield Town   **B** Rotherham United   **C.** Scunthorpe United.

6. Bob Kelly was transferred to Sunderland in 1925 for a record fee of.

   A. £4,500.   **B.** £ 5,500.   **C.** £6,500.

7. Danny Ings was signed from which club in August 2011?

   A. Bristol City.   **B.** AFC Bournemouth.   **C.** Swindon Town.

8. Who were Burnley's Charity Shield opponents in their 1–0 victory in August 1973?

   A. Everton.   **B.** Blackburn Rovers.   **C.** Manchester City.

9. At the beginning of the 1900–01 season, Burnley changed their playing strip to?

   A. Claret and Amber stripes.   **B.** Red and White.   **C.** Green and White.

10. Burnley Goalkeeper Tom Heaton at the beginning of the 2015–16 season was the first keeper at the club to become permanent club captain.

    A. False.   **B.** True.

Quiz 5

1. In January 2017, which midfielder become the clubs most expensive purchase?

   A. Steven Defour.   **B.** Jeff Hendrick.   **C.** Robbie Brady.

2. Goalkeeper Paul Robinson became the 90th Burnley goalkeeper to have made a senior appearance.

   A. True.   **B.** False.

3. Goalkeeper Tom Heaton was signed by Burnley in July 2013 from Bristol City, who had been his previous Club?

   A. Cardiff City.   **B.** Manchester United.   **C.** Royal Antwerp.

4. How many Burnley players were selected for their national sides in the 2015–16 season?

   A. 2.   **B.** 3.   **C.** 5.

5. Burnley suffered 8 consecutive League defeats in the 1994–95 season, when was the last time that they suffered 7 consecutive defeats?

   A. 1892–93. **B.** 1893–94. **C.** 1894–95.

6. In which season was a Football League fixture first televised live from Turf Moor?

   A. 1993–94.   **B.** 1994–95.   **C.** 1995–96.

7. Who replaced Burnley manager John Bond at the beginning of the 1984–85 season?

   A. Brian Miller.   **B.** Martin Buchan.   **C.** John Benson.

8. When the Bob Lord stand was opened on 14 September 1974, who were Burnley's League opponents?

   A. Blackburn Rovers.   **B.** Everton.   **C.** Leeds United.

9. In which season was Burnley captain Jimmy Adamson voted footballer of the year?

   A. 1959–60.   **B.** 1960–61.   **C.** 1961–62.

10. How many goals did leading League goalscorer Ray Pointer score in the 1961–62 season?

   A. 25.   **B.** 26.   **C.** 27.

Quiz 6

1. Who were the first two Burnley players to play together for England?

   A. Bob Kelly and Gerry Dawson.   **B.** Billy Elliott and Brian Pilkington.
   C. Jack Hill and Louis Page.

2. Which Burnley player has won the most England caps as of March 2022 ?

   A. Jack Bruton.   **B.** Martin Dobson.   **C.** Bob Kelly.

3. Which Football League side was leading Burnley goalscorer Harry Potts transferred to in October 1950?

   A. Arsenal.   **B.** Wolverhampton Wanderers.   **C.** Everton.

4. Which European side eliminated Burnley from the Inter-Cities Fairs Cup in 1967.

   A. Hamburg.   **B.** Napoli.   **C.** Eintracht Frankfurt .

5. How many League goals did Burnley concede in the 1946–47 Second Division promotion season?

   A. 29.   **B** 31.   **C.** 33.

6. How many league goals did Andy Payton score in the 1999–2000 League Division Two promotion season. ?

   A. 24.   **B.** 26.   **C.** 27.

7. Jack Butterfield was the only player signed by Burnley in the 1947–48 season?

   A. True.   **B** False.

8. In the 1981–82 Division three promotion season, leading league goalscorer Billy Hamilton scored how many goals?

   A. 10.   **B.** 11.   **C.** 13.

9. In the Second Division promotion season of 1912–13. Leading League goalscorer Bert Freeman scored how many goals?

   A. 31.   **B.** 33.   **C.** 34.

10. When was the first time that Burnley played extra time in the FA Cup?

    A. 1891.   **B.** 1895.   **C** 1915.

Quiz 7

1. Who was the first Burnley player to score a penalty in an FA Cup tie?

   A. Jimmy Ross.   **B.** Sandy Lang.   **C.** William Bury.

2. Who was the first Burnley player to score a penalty in the Football League Cup competition?

   A John Talbut.   **B.** Andy Lochhead.   **C** Willie Irvine.

3. What occupation was Burnley ex-chairman Bob Lord involved in?

   A. Fishmonger.   **B.** Greengrocer.   **C.** Butcher,

4. Which Football club did record outgoing £1.5 million player Richard Chaplow join in January 2005?

   A. Birmingham City.   **B.** Norwich City.   **C.** West Bromwich Albion,

5. What year did Burnley FC become professional?

   A. 1882.   **B**. 1883.   **C.** 1895

6. Who became the first Burnley player to become the record signing and become the clubs record outgoing signing a year later?

   A. Tony Morley.   **B.** Steven Fletcher.   **C.** Robbie Blake.

7. Which country did Maxwel Cornet play for at under 21 level?

   A. Italy.   **B.** Ivory Coast.   **C.** France.

8. How many Burnley players made international appearances throughout the 2016–17 season?

   A. 8.   **B.** 10.   **D.** 12

9. What milestone did Burnley reach in the Premier League game at Turf Moor on 8 February 2022.

   A. 5,000th.   **B.** 5,500th.   **C.** 5.750th.

10. When Burnley manager Sean Dyche was sensationally dismissed from his post on 15 April 2022, how many months and years had he been Manager?

    A. 8 years 6 months.   **B.** 9 years 3 months.   **C.** 9 years 6 months.

Quiz 8

1. Goalkeeper Colin McDonald made his League debut in April 1954 against which club?

    A. Sunderland.   **B.** Everton.   **C.** Aston Villa.

2. When Burnley narrowly avoided relegation to non-league football in 1987, who was the club that finally lost their League position?

    A. Torquay United.   **B.** Rochdale.   **C.** Lincoln City.

3. Record Burnley signing Robbie Brady who signed from Norwich City in 2017 was previously with which club?

    A. Stoke City.   **B.** Hull City.   **C.** Everton.

4. Which football club did Alex Elder join from Burnley in 1967?

    A. Everton.   **B.** Arsenal.   **C.** Stoke City.

5. How many goals did Burnley and England international Billy Elliott score against Belgium at Wembley in November 1952?

    A. None.   **B.** 1.   **C.** 2.

6. How many international goals did Jimmy McIlroy score for Northern Ireland whilst at Burnley. ?

    A. 10.   **B.** 11.   **C.** 12.

7. Both Ray Pointer and John Connelly scored for England in the World Cup qualifier in 1961 against which Nation?

    A. Luxembourg.   **B.** Italy.   **C** Portugal.

8. Who were Burnley's non-League opponents in the third round of the FA Cup at Turf Moor in January 2002?

   A. Telford United.   **B.** Harrogate Town.   **C.** Canvey Island.

9. Who Burnley's first FA Cup opponents proceeding the Second World War?

   A. Charlton Athletic.   **B.** Stoke City.   **C.** Coventry City.

10. In 1952, Burnley full-back Arthur Woodruff became the second oldest player to play for the Club?

   A. True.   **B.** False.

Quiz 9

1. How many times was Louis Page Burnley's leading League goalscorer?

   A. 1.   **B.** 2.   **C.** 3.

2. Who was the first player to score a hat-trick on his League debut?

   A. .Tom Nicol.   **B.** Claude Lambie.   **C.** Billy Bowes.

3. Who was the first Burnley player to score a hat-trick as substitute In a senior match?

   A. Ian Moore.   **B.** Gareth Taylor.   **C.** Andy Payton.

4. Record £1.million purchase Ian Moore came to Burnley from which League club?

   A. Bury.   **B.** Rochdale.   **C.** Stockport County.

5. How many League goals did leading League goalscorer Eric Probert score in the 1970–71 season?

   A. 5.   **B.** 7.   **C.** 9.

6. How many League appearances did goalkeeper Jerry Dawson make for Burnley?

   A. 520.   **B** 522.   **C.** 526.

7. Burnley went how many consecutive league games without defeat in the 1920-21 season?

   A. 28.   **B.** 30.   **C.** 32.

8. Who was Burnley's first ever substitute in a senior game?

    A. Ian Towers.   **B,** Sammy Todd.   **C.** Willie Irvine.

9. How many times has a Burnley goalkeeper scored in a senior game?

    A. Once.   **B.** Twice.   **C.** Never.

10. Who was the first substitute to come on for Burnley in the 2008–09 play-off final at Wembley against Sheffield United?

    A. Chris Eagles.   **B.** Jay Rodriguez.   **C.** Joey Gudjonsson.

Quiz 10

1. When Burnley were relegated from Division One in the 1929–30 season, which other club came down with them?

   A. Everton.   **B.** Grimsby Town.   **C.** Sheffield United.

2. What year was the new cricket field stand opened?

   A. 1969.   **B.** 1972.   **C.** 1975

3. Prior to Johann Gudmundsson's 2018 World Cup appearances in Russia for Iceland, who was the last to achieve this feat?

   A. Colin McDonald.   **B.** Jimmy McIlroy.   **C.** Billy Hamilton.

4. How many Burnley players in total have played in the World Cup Finals?

   A. 2.   **B.** 4.   **C.** 6.

5. How many goals have been scored by a Burnley player in the World Cup Finals?
   A. 1.   **B.** 2.   **C** . 3.

6. Prior to Burnley's Europa league game against Aberdeen in the 2018–19 competition, when was the last time these two clubs met?

   A. 1925.   **B.** 1927.   **C.** 1930.

7. When goalkeeper Adam Blacklaw signed for Burnley in 1954, which other club showed interest?

A. Rangers.   **B.** Dundee.   **C.** Aberdeen.

8. Dougie Newlands was the first ever Burnley player to have been signed from Aberdeen in what season?

    A. 1954–55.   **B.** 1956–57.   **C.** 1959–60.

9. Who was Burnley's first Scottish manager?

    A. Owen Coyle.   **B.** Frank Hill.   **C.** Tom Bromilow.

10. Who were the second Scottish side to play at Turf Moor?

    A. Cowlairs.   **B.** Kilmarnock.   **C.** Glasgow Northern.

Quiz 11

1. Who was the first Burnley goalkeeper to save a penalty?

   A. Alexander Kaye.   **B.** Jack Hillman.   **C.** William Cox.

2. In the 1891–92 season which league club conceded a total of 15 goals from both fixtures?

   A Stoke.   **B.** Sunderland.   **C.** Darwen.

3. Who were Burnley's league opponents in the record breaking away win in the 1891–92 season?

   A. Everton.   **B.** Sunderland.   **C.** Darwen.

4. What connections did Jay Rodriguez's dad previously have with Burnley?

   A. He was second team trainer.   **B.** He drove the team bus.
   C. He played for the reserves.

5. Who was the first Burnley player to score in a League game in the City of Manchester?

   A. William Boyd.   **B.** Robert Buchanan.   **C.** Tom Nicol.

6. Which Scottish club did Andy Payton play for?

   A. St Mirren.   **B.** Aberdeen.   **C.** Celtic.

7. 1950's legends, Albert Cheesebrough, Colin McDonald, Dougie Winton, Dougie Newlands and Les Shannon all made their final appearances for Burnley in which season?

   A. 1955–56.   **B.** 1957–58.   **C.** 1958–59.

8. Bobby Seith left Burnley in August 1960 for which Club?

   A. Aston Villa.   **B.** Motherwell.   **C.** Dundee.

9. Which Burnley player scored the club's 100th League goal in the 1960–61 season?

   A. Ray Pointer   **B.** Jimmy McIlroy.   **C.** Jimmy Adamson.

10. Jimmy Robson scored the 100th Wembley Cup Final goal in 1962 in the first half of play?

    A. True.   **B.** False.

Quiz 12

1 In Burnley's first League fixture following the Orient game on 9 May 1987, how many team changes were made in the following seasons opening League game at home to Colchester United on 15 August 1987?

   A. 4.   **B** 7.   **C.** 8.

2. Who scored Burnley's first ever recorded goal in the FA Cup tie at Astley Bridge on 23 October 1886 ?

   A. Danny Friel.   **B.** Jack Keenan.   **C.** Walter Place senior.

3. How many times have Burnley played at Wembley as of 30 April 2022?

   A. 5.   **B.** 6.   **C.** 7.

4. Who was the most capped goalkeeper to arrive at Burnley?

   A. Gabor Kiraly.   **B.** Tony Waiters.   **C.** Joe Hart.

5. In the 1945–46 season what was Burnley's official club strip?

   A. Claret and Blue.   **B.** White shirts and Black shorts   **C.** Claret and Blue hoops.

6. On the medals presented to Burnley's 1914 FA Cup winning side the inscription read. 1914 FA Cup winners.

   A. True.   **B.** False.

7. In the 1934–35 season, Burnley altered their strip to what design?

   A. Claret and Blue Quarters.   **B.** White shirts , Black shorts ,
   C. Blue shirts and Claret sleeves.

8. Accrington and Blackburn Rovers both played at Turf Moor before Burnley moved from Calder Vale in February 1882?

   A. True.   **B.** False.

9. Who was the only player to have made his debut for Burnley in the 1965–66 season?

   A. Dave Thomas.   **B.** Colin Blant.   **C.** Leonard Kinsella.

10. Who was Burnley's first goalkeeper to have played in a League match?

   A. Will Smith.   **B.** Fred Poland.   **C.** Robert Kaye.

Quiz 13

1. Who was Burnley football player William Lambie?

   A. The first to score a penalty for Burnley.   **B.** A Scottish international.   **C.** An imposter

2. How many goals did Bert Freeman score for England whilst at Burnley?

   A. 1.   **B.** 2.   **C.** 3.

3. In Burnley's promotion from Division Two in the 1999–2000 season, how many points did they obtain?
   A. 85.   **B.** 87.   **C.** 88.

4. Which club did Ian Moore move to in 2005?
   A. Rotherham United.   **B.** Leeds United.   **C.** Tranmere Rovers.

5. Who was leading League goalscorer in the 2002–03 season?
   A. Gareth Taylor.   **B.** Robbie Blake.   **C.** Glen Little.

6. From which football club was goalkeeper Peter Mellor purchased?

   A Fulham.   **B.** Wigan Athletic.   **C.** Witton Albion.

7. Who were Burnley's opponents in their first ever league match in the month of June?

   A. Millwall.   **B.** West Bromwich Albion.   **C.** Bury

8. Prior to April 2022, who was the last Burnley player to have scored five League goals?

   A. Paul Barnes.　　**B.** Andy Lochhead　　**C.** Willie Irvine.

9. How many FA Cup ties did Burnley play up to and including the 1947 Final Tie.
   A. 7.　**B.** 9.　　**C.** 10.

10. How many players made their League debuts in the 1946-47 season?
    A. 5.　**B.** 6.　**C.** 7.

Quiz 14

1. Who was the last Burnley player to have scored against Accrington or Accrington Stanley in a senior game?

   A. Ashley Barnes. 2016.   **B.** Billy Bowes. 1893.   **C.** Robert Buchanan 1893.

2. How many goals did Colin McDonald concede as an England international?

   A. 11.   **B.** 12.   **C.** 13.

3. Who was Burnley's top League goalscorer in the 2004-05 season with 10 goals scored?

   A. Ade Akinbiyi.   **B.** Ian Moore.   **C.** Robbie Blake.

4. Lucas Jutkiewicz was signed by Burnley in 2014 from which club ?

   A. Middlesbrough.   **B.** Hull City.   **C.** Blackpool.

5. When goalkeeper Paul Robinson came to Burnley as back up for Tom Heaton for the 2016–17 season, how many England caps did he achieve?

   A. 41.   **B.** 43.   **C.** 46.

6. Which former Prime Minister opened the new Brunshaw Road stand at Burnley in 1974?

   A. Edward Heath.   **B.** Harold Wilson.   **C.** James Callaghan.

7. Burnley goalkeeper Tom Heaton was England's 110 international keeper?

    A. True.   **B.** False.

8. In the 1998–99 season, Burnley manager Stan Ternent gave debuts to how many players?

    A. 18.   **B.** 20.   **C.** 21.

9. Who replaced Burnley outside left player Brian Pilkington midway through the 1960–61 season?
    A. Trevor Meredith.   **B.** Gordon Harris.   **C.** Ian Lawson.

10. Who was Burnley's first substitute to score a hat-trick in a League match?
    A. Gifton Noel-Williams.   **B.** Wayne Biggins.   **C.** Peter Noble.

Quiz 15

1. How many Burnley players played both prior to World War Two and after?

   A. 5.   **B.** 6.   **C.** 8.

2. Which season did Burnley lose to non-League Wimbledon?

   A. 1974–75. **B.** 1976–77.   **C.** 1979–80.

3. How many times was Burnley player Martin Dobson selected for England in the 1973–74 season?

   A. Once.   **B.** Twice.   **C.** Four Times.

4. What was the record fee Derby County paid Burnley for Leighton James in 1975–76 season?

   A. £310,000.   **B.** £375,000.   **C.** 410,000

5. Ray Pointer returned to Burnley in 1978 in what capacity?

   A. Assistant manager.   **B.** Reserve team coach.   **C.** Youth team coach.

6. Which season did Martin Dobson return to Burnley for a second time?

   A. 1979–80.   **B.** 1982–83.   **C.** 1985–86.

7. Which season did Brian Miller return to Burnley as manager for a second time?

   A. 1984–85.　**B.** 1986–87.　**C**. 1988–89

8. In which league season did Burnley lose 0–6 at Turf Moor to Hereford United?

   A. 1984–85.　**B.** 1986–87.　**C**. 1989–90.

9. How many goalkeepers did Burnley use in the 1991–92 Division Four Championship season?

   A. 3.　**B.** 5.　**C.** 7.

10. Which season did Ben Mee make his Burnley debut?

   A. 2011–12.　**B.** 2012–13.　**C.** 2014–15.

Quiz 16

1. Following Burnley's FA Cup win of 1914, in the first league game at Turf Moor on 5 September, how many team changes did they make?

   A. 3.   **B.** 4.   **C.** 5.

2. Which other club shared the ground at Turf Moor in the 1902–03 season?

   A. Burnley Ramblers.   **B.** Burnley Union Star.   **C.** Burnley Belvedere.

3. How many times was Billy Hamilton leading League goalscorer at Burnley?

   A. 2 times.   **B.** 3. times.   **C.** 4 times.

4. Complete this Burnley half back line-up in the 1900–01 season.

   A. Barron. Banister. Boyce.   **B.** Barron. Bannister. Dixon.   **C.** Barron. Bannister. Taylor?

5. Who were the first brothers to play for Burnley in a League match?

   A. David and Jonathan Walders.   **B.** Richard and Vince Overson.   **C.** Jack and William Gair.

6. Goalkeeper Alan Stevenson was transferred to Burnley in 1972 from?

A. Lincoln City   **B.** Barnsley.   **C.** Chesterfield.

7. Leading Burnley goalscorer George Beel came to Burnley from which Club in 1923?

   A. Lincoln City.   **B.** Norwich City.   **C.** Chesterfield.

8. When Burnley player Hugh Moffat missed a connection to an away League game on 26 November 1904 leaving them to play with ten men, where was the venue he was heading too ?

   A. Lincoln City.   **B.** Norwich City.   C. Chesterfield.

9. In an FA Cup second round tie at Turf Moor on 1 February, 1913 three players were immediately signed from the visiting side, these being Goalkeeper Ron Sewell and full backs. Sam Gundon, and Cliff Jones. Who was that visiting side?

   A. Gainsborough Trinity.   **B.** Glossop.   **C.** Stockport County.

10. How many times has Billy Ingham been substitute for Burnley in a League fixture?

   A. 7 times.   **B.** 10 times.   **C.** 30 times.

Quiz 17

FA Cup 1914. Quiz

1. Who scored the winning Cup Final goal against Liverpool in 1914?
   A. Teddy Hodgson.   **B.** Bert Freeman.   **C.** Tommy. Boyle.

2. If assists were awarded in this Final, which player would have earned that honour?
   A. Teddy Hodgson.   **B.** Eddie Mosscrop.   **C.** George Halley.

3. The 1914 FA Cup Final referee Herbert Bamlett was the youngest to officiate in a final?
   A. True.   **B.** False.

4. Burnley's league position at the end of that season was?
   A. 4th.   **B.** 8th.   **C.** 12th.

5. What was Burnley's full back line-up for that Final?
   A. Bamford and Jones.   **B.** Bamford and Taylor.   **C.** Jones and Taylor.

6. Who was Burnley's leading League goalscorer that season with 16?
   A. Teddy Hodgson.   **B.** Billy Nesbitt.   **C.** Bert Freeman.

7. King George V become the first monarch to attend a Cup Final?

A. True.   **B.** False.

8. How many times had the 1914 Burnley FA Cup winning side played together including the Final?

    A. 4 times.   **B.** 6 times.   **C.** 8 times.

9. Who were the League champions that season?

    A. West Bromwich Albion.   **B.** Everton.   **C.** Blackburn Rovers.

10. Who scored Burnley's winning goal in the replayed FA Cup Semi-final of 1914 against Sheffield United?

    A. Bert Freeman.   **B.** Billy Watson.   **C.** Tommy Boyle.

Quiz 18

1. Who was the first Burnley player to have scored in the month of June?

   A. Jay Rodriguez.   **B.** Billy Morris.   **C.** Peter Kippax.

2. Who was Burnley's chairman from June 1909 till March 1930?

   A. Harry Windle.   **B.** Charles Sutcliffe.   **C.** Edwin Whitehead.

3. Who was the first Burnley player to have enlisted in the services during World War One?

   A. Eddie Mosscrop.   **B.** Billy Watson.   **C.** Willie Nesbitt.

4. Who made the most appearances for Burnley during World War One?

   A. Bert Freeman.   **B.** Jerry Dawson.   **C.** Richard Lindley.

5. Who was Burnley's record signing in 1998?

   A. Andy Payton.   **B.** Marlon Beresford.   **C.** Steve Davis.

6. In 1995 who was Burnley's record sale to Luton Town?

   A. Chris Vinnicombe.   **B.** Chris Brass.   **C.** Steve Davis.

7. Who were Burnley's first Football League Cup opponents in October 1960?

   A. Cardiff City.   **B.** Brentford.   **C.** Bury.

8. In September 1951, who was Burnley's record £25.000 signing?

   A. Billy Holden.   **B.** Billy Elliott.   **C.** Jimmy McIlroy.

9. In the 1959–60 League championship season, how many times did Burnley top the League throughout?

   A Once.   **B** Twice.   **C.** Three times.

10. Who was Burnley's second England international player?

   A. James Crabtree.   **B.** Billy Bannister.   **C.** Jack Hillman.

Quiz 19

1. In Ian Wright's first four full games for Burnley in the 1999–2000 season, how many League goals did he score?

   A. None.   **B.** Two.   **C.** Four.

2. True or false. If Ian Wright had not scored the four goals in the 1999–2000 season, Burnley would have still been promoted?

   A. True.   **B.** False.

3. In which season did Burnley revert back to the original club badge?

   A. 2008–09.   **B.** 2009–10.   **C.** 2011–12.

4. Which Burnley player broke the deadlock in the 2014–15 season after the club had gone 655 minutes without scoring

   A. Marvin Sordell.   **B.** Ross Wallace.   **C.** Michael Kightley.

5. How many players were used in the 1959–60 Championship winning season?

   A. 15.   **B.** 17.   **C.** 18.

6. What was the minimum entrance fee to the 1962 FA Cup Final between Burnley and Tottenham Hotspur?

   A. 5 shillings   **B.** 6 shillings.   **C.** 7 shillings and sixpence.

7. Which current Burnley player is the longest serving as of May 2022?

A. Ben Mee.   **B.** Kevin Long.   **C.** Ashley Barnes.

8. How much did Burnley pay Barnsley for Tommy Boyle in 1911?

   £1,150.   **B.** £1,750.   **D.** £2,000.

9. In the 1912–13 season, Burnley recorded how many consecutive League wins?

        A. 8.   **B** 9.   **C.** 10.

10. Preceding the FA Cup final win over Liverpool in 1914, how many team changes were made for the season's final league fixture at Turf Moor against Bradford City two days later?

    A. 1.   **B.** 3.   **C.** 4.

Quiz 20

1. Who was the first Burnley player to score 100 League goals?
   A. Bert Freeman.   **B.** Bob Kelly.   **C.** George Beel.

2. How many penalty shootouts have Burnley been involved up to May 2022?
   A. 12.   **B.** 13.   **C** .16.

3. Which London league club did Bert Freeman play for before he joined Everton?
   A. Brentford.   **B.** Woolwich Arsenal.   **C.** Millwall.

4. Who have Burnley played most times in the Football League Cup?
   A. Blackburn Rovers.   **B.** Manchester United.   **C.** Tottenham Hotspur.

5. Which Burnley player scored 20 goals in his first 17 senior appearances in the 2012–13 season?
   A. Danny Ings.   **B.** Sam Vokes.   **C.** Charlie Austin,

6. Who was Burnley's youngest player to have played in all the European Cup ties?
   A. Alex Elder.   **B** Willie Irvine.   **C** Andy Lochhead.

7. Prior to May 2022, who was the last player to score a hat-trick for Burnley in a League game?
   A. Andre Gray.   **B.** Charlie Austin.   **C.** Martin Paterson.

8. Who was the first Burnley player to score four goals in a senior away game?

   A. Bob Kelly.   **B.** Jimmy Ross.   **C.** William Jackson.

9. How many Burnley players have had a surname beginning with Z?

   A. 1.   **B** 3.   **C.** 5.

10. Who was the first Burnley player to score at Wembley?

   A. Jack Billingham.   **B.** John Connelly.   **C.** Jimmy Robson.

Quiz 21

1. Burnley player Matej Vydra represented his country, The Czech Republic, more times in one season than any other Burnley player.

   A. True.   **B.** False.

2 How many Burnley players have had the surname Taylor?

   A. 9.   **B** 10.   **C.** 12.

3. Who was the first Burnley player to be sent off in a League game?

   A. Sandy Lang.   **B.** Alex Stewart.   **C.** Tom Nicol.

4. When Burnley changed their playing strip from Claret and Blue to White shirts and Black shorts in the 1930s, for how many league seasons were they worn?

   A. 2.   **B.** 3.   **C.** 4.

5. Who was the first Burnley goalkeeper to have conceded a penalty in a league game?

   A. William Tatham.   **B.** Archie Kaye.   **C.** Jack Hillman.

6. Who was Burnley's leading league goalscorer in the 1972–73 season?

   A. Keith Newton.   **B.** Ray Hankin.   **C.** Paul Fletcher.

7. In the 1971–72 season, Burnley recorded their lowest post war League attendance against which club?

   A. Preston North End.   **B.** Watford.   **C.** Millwall.

8. Who was the first Burnley player to have scored in the World Cup finals?

   A. Jimmy McIlroy.   **B.** John Connelly.   **C.** Billy Hamilton.

9. Which year did Burnley celebrate their 125th anniversary?

   A. 2007.   **B.** 2008.   **C.** .2010.

10. To which League Club was Burnley goalkeeper Brian Jensen transferred to at the end of the 1912–13 season?

    A. Oldham Athletic.   **B.** Rochdale.   **C.** Bury.

Quiz 22

Burnley Firsts

1. Who scored Burnley's first ever League goal?
   A. Pat Gallocher   **B.** Jack Yates.   **C.** Fred Poland.

2. Who scored Burnley's first ever League goal at Turf Moor?
   A. Fred Poland.   **B.** Jack Yates.   **C.** Alec Brady.

3. Who was the second Burnley player to score a hat-trick?
   A. William Tait.   **B.** Claude Lambie.   **C.** Tom Nicol.

4. Who was the first Burnley player to have scored four goals in a league game?
   A. Tom Nicol.   **B.** Billy Bowes.   **C.** Claude Lambie.

5. Who was the first Burnley player to score five League goals?
   A. Jimmy Ross.   **B.** Billy Bowes.   **C.** Walter Place senior.

6. Who was the first Burnley player to have scored five goals twice in senior games?
   A. Andy Lochhead.   **B.** Willie Irvine.   **C** George Beel.

7. Who was the first Burnley player to have made 100 League appearances. ?

    A. Bert Freeman.   **B.** William Bury.   **C.** Sandy Lang

8. Who was the first Burnley player to have scored six goals in a League game.

    A. George Beel.   **B** Louis Page.   **C.** Willie Irvine.

9. Who was the first Burnley player to have scored a goal following World War One.

    A. Bert Freeman.   **B.** Bob Kelly.   **C.** Tommy Boyle.

10. Who was the first Burnley player to have scored a goal following World War Two.

    A. Billy Morris.   **B.** Frank Kippax.   **C.** Jackie Chew.

Quiz 23

1. Which Burnley player was exchanged in a deal to bring Andy Payton to Burnley from Huddersfield Town in 1998?

   A. Kurt Nogan.   **B.** Paul Barnes.   **C.** Chris Brass.

2. How many FA Cup semi-finals have Burnley played including replays?

   A. 12. . **B.** 14.   **C.** 16.

3. How many League goals did Chris Wood score in the 2017–18 season?

   A. 8.   **B.** 9.   **C.** 10.

4. To which Football Club was Tommy Lawton transferred to in 1936?

   A. Arsenal.   **B.** Notts County.   **C.** Everton.

5. Which season did Burnley reserves first win the Central League?

   A. 1938–39.   **B.** 1946–47.   **C.** 1948–49.

6. How many hat-tricks did Harry Potts score for Burnley?
   A. 1.   **B.** 3.   **C.** 4.

7. In 1952, who became Burnley second ever oldest player?

   A. Jimmy Strong.   **B.** Harry Woodruff.   **C.** George Bray.

8. How many sets of brother have played League football for Burnley?

   A. 1.   **B.** 2.   **C.** 3.

9. Who was Burnley's longest serving Chairman?

   A. Harry Windle.   **B.** Tom Clegg.   **C.** Bob Lord.

10. Who was Burnley's first beaten opponents in the FA Cup competition?

    A. Darwen Old Wanderers.   **B.** Old Westminster's.   **C.** Accrington.

Quiz 24

1. Who was Burnley's then record £800,000 purchase in 1998?
   A. Steve Davis.　**B.** Richard Chaplow.　**C.** Robbie Blake.

2. On 19 December 1998, Burnley played their 4,000th League game against which Club?
   A. Northampton Town.　**B.** Blackpool.　**C.** Fulham.

3. Willie Morgan was transferred to Manchester United in the 1968–69 season having played how many senior games for Burnley. ?
   A 190.　**B.** 200.　**C.** 215.

4. Which Burnley player was voted runner up in the Footballer of the year award in the 1961-62 season?
   A. Jimmy Adamson.　**B.** Jimmy McIlroy.　**C.** Alex Elder.

5. What was the final score against Nottingham Forest when Jimmy Robson scored five in the 1959–60 season?
   A. 8–0.　**B.** 7–1.　**C.** 6–0.

6. How many years' service did Burnley trainer and player Charlie Bates have when he was released from contract in the 1933–34 season?
   A. 24.　**B.** 26.　**C.** 28.

7. How many penalties did record breaking taker Andy McCluggage score in all senior appearances for Burnley?
   A. 20.　**B.** 24.　**C.** 26.

8. How many penalties did the same record-breaking taker score in all League games only for Burnley?
    A. 18. **B.** 20. **C.** 22.

9. In the 1972–73 season, how many consecutive League games did Burnley remain unbeaten ?
    A. 16. **C.** 17. **D.** 18.

10. How many goals did Leighton James score for Burnley in all of his 331 plus League appearances?
    A. 60. **B.** 66. **C.** 68.

Quiz 25

1. What team did Burnley's Jay Rodriguez score four goals against in the 2011–12 seasons Football League Cup competition?

   A. Scunthorpe United.   **B.** Port Vale.   **C.** Burton Albion.

2. Who was the last player before May 2022 to have scored four goals for Burnley and not finish on the winning side?

   A. Peter Noble.   **B.** Gareth Taylor.   **C.** Willie Irvine.

3. Which Burnley full-back, who made over 500 appearances, scored four goals with two of these against Arsenal?

   A. David Taylor.   **B.** John Angus.   **C.** Len Smelt.

4. In the 1952–53 season, who became only the second Burnley player to score four in a League game following Billy Morris's four the previous season ?

   A. Billy Elliott.   **B.** Jackie Chew.   **C.** Billy Holden.

5. When Burnley purchased Turf Moor and the Cricketfield in 1922, what was the purchase price?

   A £4,500.   **B.** £4,700   **C.** £5,000.

6. Of the record breaking 188 League goals that George Beel scored for Burnley, how many FA Cup goals did he score ?

   A. 6.   **B.** 7.   **C.** 9.

7. What was Burnley author Dave Thomas's first publication?

   A. No Nay Never.   **B** Thanks for the memories.   **C.** It's Burnley not Barcelona.

8. In what season did Burnley win the Anglo-Scottish cup?

   A. 1976–77.   **B.** 1977–78.   **C** 1978–79.

9. How many England international appearances did Tommy Lawton make following his transfer from Burnley to Everton?

   A. 23.   **B.** 25.   **C.** 30.

10. How many goals did Tommy Lawton score for England?

   A. 20.   **B.** 22.   **C.** 23.

Quiz 26

1. How many Burnley players have been the club top league goalscorers four times or more?

    A. 3.   **B.** 4.   **C.** 5.

2. What was Blackburn Rovers goalkeeper Herbie Arthur's claim to fame in the league fixture at Turf Moor on 12 December 1891?

    A. He was sent off   **B.** He scored for Blackburn.   **C.** He was the only Blackburn Rovers player left on the field of play.

3. Which Burnley player scored 14 goals from 16 league games in the 1934–35 season?

    A. Eddie Hancock.   **B.** George Brown.   **C.** Jack Hornby.

4. How many League goals were scored in the record-breaking season of 1926–27?

    A. 91.   **B.** 93.   **C.** 95.

5. Owen Coyle came from St Johnstone to manage Burnley in October 2007, Which Burnley player in 1924 went from Burnley to St Johnstone to manage the Scottish side?

    A. David Taylor.   **B.** Willie Nesbitt.   C. Tommy Boyle.

6. How many Burnley players played in both the 1914 FA Cup Final and the 1921 League Championship side?

    A. 5.   **B.** 6.   **C.** 7.

7. In the record undefeated league run of 1920–21, which club ended this record undefeated run?

    A. Everton.   **B.** Manchester City.   **C.** Sunderland.

8. When was the last time a FA Cup semi-final was played at Turf Moor?

    A. 1920.   **B.** 1922.   **C.** 1924.

9. How many hat-tricks have been scored in all of Burnley's senior games up to the end of the 2021–22 season?

    A. 160.   **B.** 163   **C.** 164

10. When Burnley manager John Bond left at the end of the 1983–84 season, which club did he next manage?
    A. Swansea City.   **B.** Birmingham City.   **C.** Norwich City.

Quiz 27

1. Which Burnley player made the most ever international appearances in the 2015–16 season playing 11 times?

   A. Danny Lafferty.   **B.** Stephen Ward.   **C.** Sam Vokes.

2. How many international appearances did Michael Duff make for Northern Ireland whilst at Burnley?

   A. 21.   **B.** 23.   **C.** 25.

3. How many Burnley players were called up for International duty in the 2016–17 season?

   A. 9.   **B.** 10.   **C.** 11.

4. When Burnley goalkeeper Jimmy Strong retired from football in 1954, which profession did he undertake?

   A. Bus driver.   **B.** Pub landlord.   **C.** Poultry farmer.

5. In which English town was Burnley legend Tommy Boyle born?

   A. Bolton.   **B.** Barnsley.   **C.** Doncaster.

6. Who was the first Burnley player to have been sold for a fee of £1.25 million?

   A. Richard Chaplow.   **B.** Ade Akinbiyi.   **C.** Robbie Blake.

7. Who is Burnley's second most capped player with 40 appearances?

   A Brian Flynn.   **B.** Billy Hamilton.   **C.** Sam Vokes.

8. How many goalkeepers were used in the 2020–21 season?

   A. 3.   **B** 4.   **C.** 5.

9. In the 1956–57 season, how many goals did Ian Lawson score for Burnley in all their cup-ties?

    A. 5   **B.** 8.   **C.** 9.

10. How many Brazilian players have played for Burnley?

    A. None   **B.** 1.   **C.** 2.

Quiz 28

1. Who were Burnley's first shirt sponsor?

   A. Poco Homes.   **B**. TSB.   **C**. Endsleigh.

2. Who replaced Harry Potts in the inside-left position when he joined Everton in 1950?

   A. Jack Hays.   **B**. Billy Holden.   **C**. Jimmy McIlroy.

3. What was significant about the Preston North End goalkeeper in the Christmas Day fixture at Burnley in 1953?

   A. He was sent off.   **B**. He was brother of the Burnley keeper.
   C. He scored the winning goal.

4. As of 18 November 2020, which two Burnley goalkeepers had made 10 international appearances for their country?

   A. Danny Coyne and Colin McDonald.   **B**. Jack Hillman and Jerry Dawson   **C**. Danny Coyne and Bailey Peacock-Farrell.

5. What year was the new roof installed on the Longside?

   A. 1952.   **B**. 1953.   **C**. 1954.

6. Who was the last Burnley player to have been selected for the Football League?

   A. Gordon Harris.   **B**. Frank Casper.   **C**. Ralph Coates.

7. When Burnley legend Jimmy McIlroy won his 11th international cap for Northern Ireland, which other two Burnley players shared that landmark feat?

   A. Andy McCluggage and Bob Kelly.   **B**. Bert Freeman and Jack Hill   **C**. George Waterfield and Bob Kelly.

8. Who were Burnley's only two amateur internationals?

    A. Arthur Bell and Peter Kippax.   **B.** Jackie Chew and Peter Kippax.   **C.** Richard Twist and Arthur Bell.

9. How many of the Burnley 1967–68 FA Youth cup winning side made it as first team player.

    A. 6.   **B.** 8.   **C.** 11

10. How many times have Burnley met Blackburn Rovers in the League since 1888?

    A. 80.   **B.** 86.   **C.** 88.

Quiz 29

1. Out of the total number of league games Burnley have played from the 1888–89 season to the 2021–22 season. a total of 5,018 games, how many have been won?

   A. 1,919.   **B.** 1,921.   **C.** 1,925.

2. Out of the total number of league games Burnley have played from the 1888–89 season to the 2021–22 season. a total of 5,018 games, how many have been drawn?

   A. 1,230.   **B.** 1,234.   **C.** 1,238.

3. Out of the total number of league games Burnley have played from the 1888–89 season to the 2021–22 season. a total of 5,018 games, how many have been lost?

   A. 1,865.   **B.** 1,870.   **C.** 1,974.

4. Out of the total number of league games Burnley have played from the 1888–89 season to the 2021–22 season. a total of 5,018 games, how many goals have been scored?

   A. 7,260   **B.** 7,264.   **C.** 7,266.

5. Out of the total number of league games Burnley have played from the 1888–89 season to the 2021–22 season. a total of 5,018 games, how many goals have Been conceded?

   A. 5,712.   **B.** 5,717.   **C.** 5,720.

6. How many times have Burnley been relegated from First Division/Premier League up and including the 2021–22 season

A. 7.   **B.** 8.   **C.** 10.

7. Which was the only two seasons that Burnley finished bottom of any League?

A. 1897 and 1903.   **B.** 1900 and 1903.   **C.** 1903 and 1930.

8. Burnley in the 2021–22 season are celebrating their 140th Anniversary?

A. True.   **B.** false.

9. What was Burnley's record home Post War attendance?

A. 52,869.   **B.** 54.775.   **C.** 57,989.

10. What was the attendance for the Sherpa Van Final in 1988 at Wembley Stadium when Burnley played Wolverhampton Wanderers?

A. 60,841.   **B.** 70,841.   **C.** 80,841.

Quiz 30

1 Burnley were Wimbledon's second league opponents when they moved to Milton Keynes in 2003?

   A. True.   **B.** False.

2. Michael Kightly was transferred from Burnley to which club in August 2017?

   A. Burton Albion.   **B.** Colchester United.   **C.** Southend United.

3. When Burnley were formed in May 1882, how many games were played on their first ground, Calder Vale, before moving to Turf Moor?

   A. 11.   **B.** 21.   **C.** 23.

4. Jack Yates, Burnley's first England international, played how many league games in his career at the club?

   A. 29.   **B.** 31.   **C.** 33.

5. Who were Sean Dyche's first league opponents as Burnley manager?

   A. Leeds United.   **B.** Wolverhampton Wanderers.   **C.** Charlton Athletic.

6. When Jack Cork was first at Burnley, which club was he loaned from?

   A. Liverpool.   **B.** Everton.   **C.** Chelsea.

7. What League season did Burnley last play on Christmas Day?

    A. 1955–56.   **B.** 1956–57.   **C.** 1957–58.

8   Which club was relegated with Burnley in the 1929–30 season?

    A. Manchester City.   **B.** Everton.   **C.** Sunderland.

9. How many seasons did Jimmy Mullen have at Burnley?

    A. 3.   **B.** 4.   **C.** 5.

10. Who were Burnley's opponents in the final league game before World War Two?

    A. Birmingham.   **B.** Coventry City.   **C.**   Bradford City.

Quiz 31

1. Around which time were Burnley first called the Clarets?
   A. 1960s.   **B** 1970s.   **C.** 1980s.

2. In the early days, Burnley played two games at the same time.
   A. True.   **B** False.

3. Goalkeeper Jimmy Strong was signed from which club in 1946?
   A. West Bromwich Albion   **B.** Portsmouth.   **C.** Walsall.

4. In which season did Burnley first participate in the Anglo Scottish Cup competition?
   A. 1974–75.   **B.** 1975–76.   **C.** 1976–77.

5. Who was Burnley's first recorded goalkeeper to play in a senior fixture?
   A. Robert Kay.   **B.** James McConnell.   **C.** William Smith.

6. Who was the leading league goalscorer in the 1938–39 season with 10 goals?
   A. James Clayton.   **B.** Bob Brocklebank.   **C.** Billy Morris.

7. Who is Burnley's second highest league goalscorer with 118 goals?
   A. Jimmy McIlroy.   **B.** Andy Lochhead.   **C.** Ray Pointer.

8. What is the highest score that Burnley have beaten Blackburn Rovers by at Turf Moor?

   A. 5–1.   **B.** 6–0.   **C.** 7–1.

9. Burnley have won all four divisional titles. Which two other clubs share this feat?

   A. Wolverhampton Wanderers and Preston North End.   **B.** Bury and Preston North End   **C.** Wolverhampton Wanderers and Bury.

10. Who was Burnley's record buy in 1938 from Aston Villa?

    A. Bob Brocklebank.   **B.** Billy Morris.   **C.** James Clayton.

Quiz 32

1. How many times has Steve Kindon been Burnley's top league goalscorer?

   A. none.   **B.** Once.   **C.** Twice.

2. In the World Cup Qualifier in Cardiff on 9 October 2017 between Wales and the Republic of Ireland, how many Burnley players were involve?

   A. 2.   **B.** 3.   **C.** 5.

3. Burnley's last league victory at Everton was on 1 October 2017, in what season was the previous league victory at Goodison Park?

   A 1966–67.   **B.** 1973–74.   **C.** 1975–76.

4. Who were Burnley's opponents when Prince Albert Victor (Queen Victoria's grandson) attended Turf Moor on 13 October 1886?

   A. Bolton Wanderers.   **B.** Preston North End.   **C.** Everton.

5. Which Italian side were interested in signing Jimmy McIlroy in the early nineteen sixties?

   A. Juventus.   **B.** Inter Milan.   **C.** AC Milan.

6. Which Burnley player scored a total of 189 goals in all senior appearances?

   A. Ray Pointer.   **B.** George Beel.   **C.** Andy Lochhead.

7. Which player has scored the most hat-tricks for Burnley in all senior appearances?

    A. Bert Freeman.   **B.** Andy Lochhead.   C George Beel.

8. Which Burnley book was the first to have a QR code in it so some parts of it could be downloaded?

    A. Dave Thomas's *Bob Lord of Burnley*.   **B.** Mike Prosser's. *Burnley Goalkeeping Legends.*   **C.** Tim Quelchs *From the Orient to the Emirates.*

9. Albanian international Besart Berisha, who represented his country ten times whilst at Burnley, played how many time for the club?

    A. Twice.   **B.** Four times.   **C.** Never.

10. How many hat-tricks did Tommy Lawton score for Burnley?

    A. None.   **B.** One.   **C.** Two.

Quiz 33

1. Who was Burnley's first ex-player to be appointed manager of the club?

   A. Cliff Britton.   **B**. Alan Brown.   **C**. Harry Potts.

2. How many League fixtures did Burnley lose in the Championship season of 1959–60?

   A. 9.   **B**. 11.   **C**. 13.

3. How many full seasons did Cliff Britton have as Burnley manager?

   A. 1.   **B**. 2.   **C**. 3.

4. How many Burnley players made debuts in the opening Championship game at Huddersfield Town on 29 July 2022.

   A. 6.   **B**. 7.   **C**. 8.

5. In which season did Burnley record their first goalless League game?

   A. 1988–89.   **B**. 1889–90.   **C**. 1891–92.

6. Chairman Alan Pace took over the Chairman's roll at Burnley in December 2020. He was the 19th to do so.

   A. . True.   **B**. False.

7. How many Burnley players appeared in all 42 League games in the Championship winning season of 1920-21?

   A. 1.   **B.** 3.   C. 5.

8. When was the old Longside demolished?

   A. September 1994.   **B.** September 1995.   **B.** August 1996.

9. Where does super fan Dave Burnley come from?

   A. Manchester.   **B.** Stoke-on-Trent.   **C.** Burnley.

10. Jimmy McIlroy and John Angus both share the same number of league appearances, how many games?

    A. 425.   **B.** 435.   **C.** 439.

Quiz 34

1. Burnley manager, Vincent Kompany, who was appointed in June 2022 was the 28th permanent manager.

   A. True.   **B.** False.

2. Which Burnley manager had the shortest reign.

   A. Billy Dougall.   **B.** John Benson.   **C.** Martin Buchan.

3. Who was Burnley's first full-time Manager .

   A. Harry Bradshaw.   **B.** Ernest Mangnall.   **C.** Spencer Whittaker.

4. Who was the first player to score a league goal against Burnley?

   A. Jimmy Ross   **B.** Fred Dewhurst.   **C.** Jack Drummond

5. Which season did Burnley have their longest ever winning run?

   A. 1912–13.   **B.** 1914–15.   **C.** 1920–21.

6. Who was the first Burnley player to have scored for the club in a European Cup tie?

   A. Jimmy McIlroy.   **B.** Brian Miller   **C.** Gordon Harris

7. Who was Burnley's record £ 400,000 signing in 1996?

   A. Nigel Gleghorn.   **B.** Glen Little.   **C.** Paul Barnes.

8. What was significant about the date 29 November 1919 in Burnley's history?

A. Burnley's first ever gate of 50,000.   **B.** Bert Freeman's 100th League goal.

C. Burnley topped the First Division for the second time in the club's history.

9.   Who were Burnley's League opponents when a League game ended with an aggregate of ten goals at Turf Moor on 4 November 1922?

A. Blackburn Rovers.   **B**. West Bromwich Albion.   **C.** Nottingham Forest.

10. How many European cup ties have Burnley played in total?

A. 16.   **B.** 18.   **C.** 20.

Quiz 35

1. Who was the first Burnley manager to have had First Division playing experience?

   A. Harry Potts.　　**B.** Cliff Britton.　　**C.** Tom Bromilow.

2. Who was the last Burnley player to have been selected for international duty prior to the outbreak of the Second World War?

   A. Tommy Willighan.　　**B.** Jack Hill.　　**C.** Andy McCluggage.

3. How many League appearances did full-back Ben Mee make for Burnley?

   A. 351.　　**B.** 361.　　**C.** 372.

4. Which Northern Ireland player was capped for his country five days after making his debut for Burnley?

   A. Tommy Willighan.　　**B.** Hugh Flack.　　**C.** Billy Hamilton.

5. Which League club did Tom Bromilow join following his resignation from Burnley in 1935?

   A. Arsenal.　　**B.** Fulham.　　**C.** Crystal Palace.

6. Prior to May 2022, which was the last Burnley player to have scored on his Premier League debut. ?

   A. Ashley Barnes.　　**B.** Jimmy Dunne.　　**C.** Jay Rodriguez.

7. When Paul Barnes scored five league goals against Stockport County in the 1996–97 season, how many other Burnley players have achieved this feat in a League match?

   A. 4.　　**B.** 5.　　**C.** 6.

8. In the 2006–07 season, how many League games did Burnley go without a league win?

   A. 18.   **B.** 20.   **C.** 22.

9. In which season was Jay Rodriguez first top league goalscorer?

   A. 2008–09.   **B.** 2009–10.   **C.** 2010–11.

10. In the 2016-17 season, which player became the first Burnley player to be capped for England since 1974?

    A. Michael Keane.   **B.** Tom Heaton.   **C.** Nick Pope.

Quiz 36

1. Alex Leake who joined Burnley in 1907 won how many England caps with his previous Club Aston Villa?

   A. 3.   **B.** 5.   **C.** 8.

2. Spencer Whittaker, joined Burnley and became their third manager. Which season was this?

   A. 1903–04.   **B.** 1905–06.   **D.** 1908–09.

3. What was the winning score of Burnley's Qualifying third round encounter at Keswick In October 1903. ?

   A. 6–0.   **B.** 7–0.   **C.** 8–0.

4. Burnley's FA Cup opponents Bury beat them 1–0 at Turf Moor on 27 January 1900 in the first round, how much further did they go In this competition?

   A. Semi-Finals.   **B.** Beaten Finalists. **C.** FA Cup winners.

5. In January 1906, which Burnley player made his 300th League appearance?

   A. Joe Taylor.   **B.** Arthur Dixon.   **C.** Billy Bannister.

6. Who became Burnley's record-breaking top scorer in the 1907–08 season with 24 goals?

   A. Dugald McFarlane.   **B.** Hugh Moffat.   **C.** Dick Smith.

7. In the 1900–01 season Burnley played both Newton Heath and Small Heath in the FA Cup rounds of that season. If the ties were played today, what would both clubs be renamed?

    A. Manchester City and Birmingham City. **B.** Manchester United and West Bromwich Albion. **C.** Manchester United and Birmingham City.

8. Who were the opponents in Jack Hillman's last ever game for Burnley, an FA Cup tie on 25 January 25 1902?

    A. At Bishop Auckland. **B.** At Bury. **C.** At Walsall.

9. Which Football League Club did goalkeeper Jack Hillman join in January 1902.?

    A. Dundee. **B.** Manchester City **C.** Oldham Athletic.

10. Where was Burnley's leading league goalscorer of both the 1901–02 and 1902–03 seasons Cornelius Hogan born?

    A. England. **B.** Scotland **C.** Malta.

Quiz 37

1. What do passed Burnley players Dick Smith, Bert Freeman and George Beel have in common?

   A. They all scored on their Burnley debuts.   **B.** They all moved to Lincolnshire.

   C. They were all club record goalscorers.

2. Who was Burnley's record £1,150 signing in the 1911–12 season?

   A. Billy Watson.   **B.** Tommy Boyle.   **C.** Willie Nesbitt.

3. How many goals did Burnley score in their winning FA Cup campaign of 1913–14 in including the final?

   A. 13.   **B.** 15.   **C.** 17.

4. What was the attendance for the FA Cup Final of 1914 at Crystal Palace?

   A. 72,776.   **B.** 82,776.   **C.** 90,776.

5. How many goals did Burnley score in their League cup ties of the 1982–83 season that took them to the semi-final?

   A. 18.   **B.** 20.   **C.** 22.

6. Since 1885, how many FA Cup winners have beaten Burnley in all rounds including the Semi Finals and Final?

   A. 11.   **B.** 13.   **C.** 15.

7. Since 1961, how many Football League Cup winners have beaten Burnley in all rounds including the Semi-Finals ?

    A. 5.   **B**. 6.   **C**. 7.

8. On 29 March 2022, Burnley set a new record when three goalkeepers played for their national sides at the same time.

    A. True.   **B.** False.

9. When Billy Morris was selected for Wales in April 1947, how many years had it been since a Burnley player was last selected for his national side?

    A. 12.   **B.** 14.   **C.** 16.

10. When Burnley became founder members of the Football league in 1888, how many other east Lancashire sides joined them?

    A. 2.   **B.** 3.   **D.** 4.

Quiz 38

1. In the 2009–10 Premiership season, how many goals did top league goalscorer Steven Fletcher score?

    A. 7.   **B.** 8.   **C.** 10.

2. How many full league appearances did Paul Gascoigne make in the 2001–02 season?

    A. 3.   **B.** 4.   **C.** 5.

3. In which season did Frank Teasdale take over as Chairman of Burnley FC?

    A. 1982–83.   **B.** 1984–85.   C. 1986–87.

4. Which year did Ex Chairman Bob Lord pass away?

    A. 1981.   **B.** 1983.   **C.** 1985.

5. How many goals did Burnley goalkeeper Billy O'Rourke concede during his Burnley debut on 27 October 1979 at Queen's Park Rangers?

    A. 5.   **B.** 6.   **C.** 7.

6. When Burnley lost to Swindon Town in the third round of the FA Cup on 10 January 1948, which ex-Burnley player managed them?

    A. George Beel.   **B.** Louis Page.   **C.** Bob Brocklebank.

7. When Burnley manager Frank Hill resigned in the 1954–55 season, which club did he go on to manage?

   A. Preston North End.　　**B.** West Bromwich Albion.　　**C.** Huddersfield Town.

8. Who was the first Burnley player to have scored a hat-trick on his league debut?

   A. Claude Lambie.　　**B.** Tom Nicol.　　**C.** Alec Brady.

9. Who was the first Burnley player to have score two successive League hat-tricks?

   A. Walter Place senior　　**B.** Tom Nicol.　　**C.** Claude Lambie.

10. When Jimmy McIlroy left Burnley for Stoke in 1963, which other player also left at the same time?

   A. Tommy Cummings.　　**B.** Ray Pointer.　　**C.** Brian Pilkington.

Quiz 39

1. Which league club did full-backs David Holt and Ian Wood play for before signing for Burnley in the 1980–81 season?

   A. Rochdale.   **B.** Bury.   **C.** Oldham Athletic.

2. In which Football League season did awarding three points for a win start?

   A. 1981–82.   **B.** 1983–84.   **C.** 1987–88.

3. Which non-League club held Burnley to a goalless draw at Turf Moor in a first-round tie on 21 November 1981?

   A. Altrincham.   **B.** Runcorn.   **C.** Accrington Stanley.

4. Which Burnley player was transferred to Aston Villa in 1979 for a fee of £220,000?

   A. Tony Morley.   **B.** Phil Cavener.   **C.** Terry Cochrane.

5. When Willie Irvine equalled Jimmy Robson's record 37 goals in the 1965–66 season, how many international goals did he score for Northern Ireland in the same season?

   A. None.   **B.** Two.   **C.** Four.

6. Which first division club beat Burnley in the FA Cup Semi-final of the 1934–35 season?

   A. Arsenal.   **B.** Newcastle United.   **C.** Sheffield Wednesday.

7. Which club did Burnley legend Jack Bruton sign for in December 1929?
   A. Manchester City. **B.** Blackburn Rovers. **C.** Bolton Wanderers.

8. Which Burnley goalkeeper reached 172 consecutive league appearances on 15 March 1965 at Elland Road against Leeds United
   A. Harry Thomson. **B.** Des Thompson. **C.** Adam Blacklaw.

9. What was the fee when Ralph Coates was transferred to Tottenham Hotspur in May 1971?
   A. £190,000. **B.** £ 220,000. **C.** 235,000.

10. Which season was the new Club crest introduced that replaced the one with the letters B F C.?
    A. 1978–79. **B.** 1979–80. **C.** 1981–82.

Quiz 40

1. Who was the first non-league club to have knocked Burnley out of the FA Cup after 1888?

   A. Small Heath.　　**B.** Sheffield United.　　**C.** Notts County.

2. How many full-time managers have managed Burnley twice?

   A. 1.　　**B.** 2.　　**C.** 3.

3. Burnley's league fixture against Coventry City was abandoned due to the declaring of the Second World War in August 1939, The fixture was resumed in August 1946, how many Burnley players played in both?

   A. 2.　　**B.** 5.　　**C.** 7.

4. When did Burnley Secretary Charles Sutcliffe become Club Chairman?

   A. January 1883.　　**B.** March 1898.　　**C.** May 1896.

5. Tom Morrison was the second Burnley player to have been capped by Northern Ireland?

   A. True.　　**B.** False.

6. How long was Burnley goalkeeper Jack Hillman suspended for following his attempted bribe to the Nottingham Forest players at Trent Bridge in April 1900?

   A. Six months.　　**B.** One Year.　　**C.** Indefinite .

7. What was Burnley's colours before they wore the green and white strip in 1900?

    A. Red and White.   **B.** Claret and Gold.   **C.** Pink and White stripes.

8. Who were the first London league club that Burnley defeated?

    A. Woolwich Arsenal.   **B.** Brentford.   **C.** Clapton Orient.

9. In the 1925–26 League season, how many games did Burnley lose by conceding six goals or more?

    A. 5.   **B.** 6.   **C.** 8.

10. When was the first Burnley supporters club formed?

    A. 1927.   **B.** 1929.   **C.** 1932.

Quiz 41

1 How many Burnley players appeared in both the 2013–14 and 2015–16 promotion winning seasons?

   A. 7.   **B.** 8.   **C.** 9.

2. Prior to the 2017–18 season, when was the last season that Burnley didn't score from the penalty spot?

   A. 1963–64.   **B.** 1965–66.   **C.** 1967–68.

3. How many penalties did Graham Alexander score in the 2008–09 season?

   A. 7.   **B.** 9.   **C.** 11.

4. World War Two goalkeeper Harry Holdcroft conceded a record 13 goals in a friendly against which side.

   A. Bolton Wanderers.   **B.** Blackpool.   **C.** Bury.

5. From which club did Ian Britton sign for Burnley in August 1986?

   A. Blackpool.   **B.** Bolton Wanderers. **C.** Shrewsbury Town.

6. How many Burnley players appeared in all of the 42 league games of the 1946–47 promotion winning season?

   A. 1.   **B.** 3   **C.** 5.

7. Who scored Burnley's first ever League Cup goal?

   A. John Connelly.   **B.** Ray Pointer.   **C.** Gordon Harris.

8. In the inaugural 1st season that Burnley played in 1888–89, how many players appeared in all 22 League games?

    A. None.   **B.** 1.   **C.** 3.

9. In which season did Burnley make their 2,000 top tier League appearance?

    A. 2009–10.   **B.** 2014–15.   **C.** 2020–21.

10. The trophy that Burnley won in the 2015–16 Championship season was the same trophy that they won in 1921 and 1960.

    A. True.   **B.** False.

Quiz 42

1. How many times in the history of Burnley Football Club have they been automatically promoted?

   A. 5.   **B.** 6.   **C.** 8.

2. How many times have Burnley been promoted through the play-off system?

   A. 2.   **B.** 3.   **C.** 4.

3. Prior to the 2014–15 season, when was the last time that Burnley had three consecutive 0–0 drawn League games?

   A. 1928-29.   **B.** 1931-32.   **C.** Never.

4. In the promotion winning season of 2013–14 , how many Burnley players appeared in all 46 League games?

   A. 2.   **B.** 3.   **C.** 4.

5. Which two clubs were relegated with Burnley in the 2009–10 season?

   A. Wolverhampton Wanderers and Portsmouth.   **B.** Crystal Palace and Hull City.   **C.** Portsmouth and Hull City.

6. In the 1994–95 season, Burnley equalled their record of how many straight defeats?

   A. 6.   **B.** 7.   **C.** 8.

7. In the 1991-92 Division 4 Championship winning season, how many players made all 42 appearances ?
   A. None.   B. 2.   **C.** 4.

8. Who was the first Burnley player to score five goals in the FA Cup?
   A. Ray Pointer.   **B.** Jimmy Robson.   **C.** Andy Lochhead.

9. Which Burnley player has recorded the most appearances for his country prior to 2005 with 64 appearances, 34 of which were whilst playing for Burnley?
   A. Jimmy McIlroy.   **B.** Willie Irvine.   **C.** Brian Flynn.

10. Who was the first Burnley player to have scored seven goals in consecutive league games?
    A. Andy Lochhead.   **B.** Willie Irvine.   **C.** Charlie Austin.

Quiz 43

1. Which league season did Burnley start with no wins from the first 16 games?

    A. 1979–80.   **B.** 1982–83.   **C.** 1986–87

2. How many appearances for Burnley did Michael Duff make in all senior Games?

    A. 351.   **B.**   355.   **C.** 383.

3. Which league club approached Jimmy Adamson for the position of manager before he was appointed by Burnley?

    A. Sunderland.   **B.** Leeds United.   **C.** Bolton Wanderers.

4. Why were Burnley refused entry into the Inter-Cities Fairs Cup competition in 1963?

    A. Turf Moor ground was deemed unsafe.   **B.** Burnley did not have enough foreign players.   **C.** Burnley was not a city.

5. Burnley legend Tommy Boyle left Burnley in 1922 he went on to play for which Welsh side?

    A. Wrexham.   **B.** Swansea Town.   **C.** Newport County.

6. Which club defeated Burnley in the third round of the FA Cup in the Championship winning season of 1920–21?

    A. Fulham.   **B.** Tottenham Hotspur.   **C.** Hull City.

7. Who was the first foreign player to represent Burnley in a League game?

   A. Cornelius Hogan.   **B.** Max Seeburg. **C.**   Pat Gallocher.

8. How many times was Burnley legend Jimmy McIlroy leading league goal scorer?

   A. Twice.   **B.** 3 times.   **C.** Never.

9. Who were Jimmy McIlroys final league game opponents against Burnley?

   A. Everton.   **B.** Sheffield Wednesday.   **C.** Sheffield United.

10. What other non-league club is known as the Clarets?

   A. Altrincham.   **B.** Chelmsford City.   **C.** Baldock Town.

Quiz 44

1. In which season did Burnley win the FA Youth cup?

    A. 1963–64.   **B.** 1966–67.   **C.** 1967–68

2. In the epic five FA Cup ties that Burnley played against Chelsea in 1956, how many goals did Burnley score?

    A. 4.   **B.** 5.   **C.** 6.

3. Who was the first Burnley player to have scored at West Bromwich Albion?

    A. Pat Gallocher.   **B.** Will Tait.   **C.** Jack Yates.

4. Who holds Burnley's post war league scoring record with 29?

    A. Willie Irvine.   **B.** Andy Lochhead.   **C.** Jimmy Robson.

5. Which was the first league season that Burnley conceded over 100 goals?

    A. 1922–23.   **B.** 1925–26.   **C.** 1928–29.

6. Who were Eddie Howe's first league opponents as manager at Burnley?

    A. Wolverhampton Wanderers.   **B.** Birmingham City.   **C.** Scunthorpe United.

7. When Burnley lost to Charlton Athletic in the 1946–47 FA Cup Final, how many more league games were left to fulfil?

    A. 6.   **B.** 7.   **C.** 8.

8. When Burnley narrowly avoided relegation to non-league football in 1987, which club was promoted to the Football League that season?

   A. Barnet.　　**B.** Scarborough. **C.** Maidstone United.

9. In the promotion winning season of 1999–2000, how many Burnley players made all 46 appearances?

   A. None.　　**B.** 1.　　**C.** 3.

10. How many Burnley players, prior to World War Two had played for England?

   A. 12.　　**B.** 14.　　**C.** 16.

Quiz 45

1972-73 Second Division Winning Season

1. How many of the 1973 Second Division Championship team played in all 42 games?

   A. 6.   **B.** 7.   **C.** 8.

2. Which Burnley player was sold to Queens Park Rangers having played the first eleven games that season?

   A. Arthur Bellamy.   **B.** Peter Mellor.   **C.** Dave Thomas.

3. How many players made their debut that season?

   A. 1.   **B.** 2.   **C.** 4.

4. Burnley, who were invited to play in the Charity Shield final having been 1972–73 Second Division Champions, played Manchester City at Main Road in the August of 1973, who scored the goal that won them the game?

   A. Paul Fletcher.   **B.** Colin Waldron.   **C.** Ray Hankin.

5. Who was the leading league goalscorer that season with 15 goals scored?

   A. Frank Casper.   **B.** Paul Fletcher.   **C.** Leighton James.

6. What was the previous season that Burnley were Champions of the Second Division?

   A. 1884–85.   **B.** 1897–98.   **C.** 1912–13.

7. How many games were lost throughout that season?

    A. 4.   **B**. 6.   **C.** 8.

8. How many games did Burnley remain unbeaten at the start of that season.

    A. 14.   **B.** 16.   **C.** 18.

9. Who's testimonial match that season attracted an attendance of 2,000 more than the average attendance at the home league games that season. ?

    A. Ray Pointer.   **B.** Colin McDonald.   **C.** John Angus,

10. How many international appearances did Leighton James make for Wales that 1972–73 season. ?

    A. 6.   **B.** 8.   **C.** 10.

Quiz 46

1. From which league club was goalkeeper Tom Heaton transferred from to Burnley?

   A. Bristol Rovers.　　**B.** AFC Bournemouth.　　**C.** Bristol City.

2. How many Football League goals did Burnley goalkeeper Tom Heaton concede in the 2013–14 season?

   A. 30.　　**B.** 36.　　**C.** 40.

3. When Tom Heaton was sent off at Brighton in the 2013–14 season, which Burnley goalkeeper took his place?

   A. Alex Cisak.　　**B.** Nick Liversedge.　　**C.** Ashley Barnes.

4. Burnley midfielder Scott Arfield, made his debut for Burnley as substitute against which Championship side in the 2013–14 season?

   A. Sheffield Wednesday.　　B. Bolton Wanderers.　　**C.** Yeovil Town.

5. How many league goals did Danny Ings score for Burnley in the 2013–14 season?

   A. 19.　　**B.** 21.　　**C.** 23.

6. How many league goals did Burnley goalkeeper Jimmy Strong concede in the 1946–47 season?

   A. 21.　　**B.** 22.　　**C.** 29.

7. Who was the first foreign player to have represented Burnley in a league game?

    A. Cornelius Hogan.   **B.** Max Seeburg.   **C.** Pat Gallocher.

8. Who is the only Burnley player to have represented the club at both Rugby and football?

    A. Will Bury.   **B.** Thomas Midgley.   **C.** Sandy Lang.

9. How many senior appearances did Burnley goalkeeper Adam Blacklaw make in the 1960–61 season?

    A. 60.   **B.** 62.   **C.** 64.

10. In 1937, Burnley were beaten 1–7 at Turf Moor by which club in the fifth round of the FA Cup?

    A. Everton.   **B.** Arsenal.   **C.** Liverpool.

Quiz 47

1. Goalkeeper Jerry Dawson made a record total of 569 senior appearances for Burnley?

   A. True.   **B.** False.

2. Who was the first Burnley manager to win promotion twice for the club.

   A. Jimmy Mullen.   **B.** Sean Dyche.   **C.** Brian Miller.

3. Who were Burnley's first London opponents?

   A. Clapton Orient.   **B.** Woolwich Arsenal.   **C.** London Scottish.

4. How many goals did Andre Gray score in the 2015–16 season in all senior appearances?

   A. 25.   **B.** 27.   **C.** 30.

5. What was the average home attendance in the 1888–89 season?

   A. 3,900.   **B.** 4,250.   **C.** 4,454.

6. Who was the second highest League hat-trick scorer with 5 hat-tricks?

   A. Bert Freeman.   **B.** Gareth Taylor.   **C.** Paul Barnes.

7. How many Burnley players who have been selected for England have scored a hat-trick?

   A. 1.   **B.** 2.   **C.** 4.

8. Which Burnley international has scored the most goals for his country?

   A. Bob Kelly.   **B.** Willie Irvine.   **C.** Jimmy McIlroy.

9. Which Burnley player has made the second most appearances with 540 senior appearances?

   A. John Angus.   **B.** Alan Stevenson.   **C.** Tommy Cummings.

10. Which Burnley player has scored the second highest total of goals in all senior appearances whilst at the club?

    A. Ray Pointer   **B.** Jimmy McIlroy.   **C.** Andy Lochhead.

Quiz 48

1. Under the old points system with two points for a win, what was the highest that Burnley gained up to the 1980–81 season?

   A. 60.   **B**. 62.   **C.** 64.

2. How many full-time managers have Burnley had up until 30 June 2022?

   A. 29.   **B.** 31.   **C.** 33.

3. Burnley players James Tarkowski and Andre Gray were signed from which London side?

   A. Millwall.   **B.** Charlton Athletic.   **C.** Brentford.

4. In the Second division winning season of 1897–98, how many Burnley players made all 30 league appearances. ?

   A. 1.   B. 3.   **C.** 5.

5. The first abandoned league game against Blackburn Rovers at Turf Moor happened in which season?

   A. 1891–92   **B.** 1893–94.   **C.** 1896–97.

6. Which was the first abandoned league game at Turf Moor because of floodlight failure?

   A. Versus Leicester City January 2005. **B.** Versus Walsall December 1996.   **C.** Versus Scarborough January 1992.

7. Which club did Burnley first beat at Turf Moor on 3 March 1883?

   A. Blackburn Olympic A side.   **B.** Accrington A side.   **C.** Great Harwood.

8. How old was goalkeeper Jerry Dawson when he won his second England cap?

   A. 30.   **B.** 32.   **C.** 34.

9. How many Burnley players made their League debut in the 1961–62 season?

   A. 1.   **B.** 3.   **C.** 5.

10. On 30 September 1961, having beaten Fulham at Craven Cottage 5–3, there were two previous away games where they recorded wins of 6–2, who were the two clubs that Burnley beat?

    A. Birmingham City and West Bromwich Albion.   **B.** Leicester City and West Bromwich Albion   **C.** Birmingham City and Leicester City.

Quiz 49

1. Who was the first Burnley player to have played for the Republic of Ireland?

   A. Keith Treacy.   **B.** Stephen Ward.   **C.** Jeff Hendrick.

2. What was Burnley goalkeeper Brian Jensen's nickname?

   A. Hulk.   **B.** The Beast.   **C.** Giant.

3. How many post war leading League goalscorers have scored 25 or more in a season?

   A. 5.   **B.** 7.   **C.** 9.

4. How many post war leading League goalscorers have scored nine or less in a season?

   A. 8.   **B.** 10.   **C.** 12.

5. Who were Burnley's shirt sponsors in the 2009–10 season?

   A. Holland's pies.   **B.** Oak Furniture   **C.** Cooke's Oil.

6. Who in 2008 was Burnley's player of the year two seasons running?

   A. Gary Cahill.   **B.** Wade Elliott.   **C.** Sam Vokes.

7. Burnley legend Peter Noble scored against them in the 1969 League Cup Semi-final for which club?

   A. Aston Villa.   **B.** Swindon Town.   **C.** Norwich City.

8. What was the result of Burnley's encounter against Aldershot on 24 August 1991 at Turf Moor that was eventually expunged owing to the club resigning from the Football League.

   A. 1–0.   B. 2–2.   **C.** 2–0.

9. When was ex-Burnley player Paul Fletcher awarded an MBE for services to football?

   A. 2007.   **B.** 2009.   **C.** 2011.

10. Which Burnley player held the record in 1911 for the most League appearances for the Club?

    A. Fred Barron.   **B.** Joe Taylor.   **C.** Hugh Moffat.

Quiz 50

1. How many League games have been played at Turf Moor on Christmas Day?

   A. 35.   **B.** 37.   **C.** 40.

2. Which Burnley player has been awarded the most international caps whilst at other clubs?

   A. Bryan Flynn.   **B.** Gabor Kiraly.   **C.** Jimmy McIlroy.

3. How many times have Burnley conceded seven goals at Turf Moor in a League game?

   A. 2.   **B.** 3.   **C.** 5.

4. How many times have Burnley conceded 10 goals in a League game?

   A. Once.   **B.** Twice.   **C.** Three times.

5. How many times have Burnley won the Lancashire Senior Cup?

   A. 9.   **B.** 11.   C. 12.

6. Burnley's popular Physiotherapist Jimmy Holland had a testimonial against which club?

   A. Wigan Athletic.   **B.** Oldham Athletic.   **C.** Rochdale.

7. Burnley's chief benefactor Charles Massey in the 1882–83 season was a?

   A. Local brewery owner.   **B.** Local pit owner.   **C.** Local licensee.

8. Scott Twine, Burnley's June 2022 signing from Milton Keynes Dons, played how many games for the Dons?

   A. 35.   **B.** 40.   **C.** 45.

9. Burnley manager Vincent Kompany who was appointed Burnley manager in June 2022 played how many senior games for Manchester City?

   A. 265.   **B.** 295   **C.** 305.

10. At the beginning of the 1973–74 First Division season. How many league games did Burnley remain unbeaten.

   A. 5.   **B.** 7.   **C.** 9.

A meeting was held at the Bull Hotel, Manchester Road, Burnley by the Burnley Rovers Rugby Club on the 18th May 1882 to discuss the change from rugby football to that of association football that was now being adopted across the land. Burnley Rovers who they were still called changed the name to just Burnley later that Summer. The committee headed by secretary Mr Waddington, treasurer Mr Baron and local brewery owner William Massey were all supportive of this change over, as were all others at the meeting.

Team line up of the Burnley team who won the Lancashire senior cup in 1889-90 From left to right. William McFettridge, William Bury, J Kearsley (umpire). Danny Spiers, Tom White (Club Secretary) Middle row. Robert Haresnape, Alex McLardie, Sandy Lang, Claude Lambie, Alex Stewart. and James Hill.
Front row. Archie Kaye and Jack Keenan

Caption inside photo: The 1893 Burnley East Lancashire Charity Cup winners.

Label inside photo: 1892-93 team group East Lancashire Charity Cup winners

Players back row left to right. Walter Place senior, J Stuttard (Trainer) Tom Nicol, James Mullineaux, Jack Hillman, Archie Livingstone, Mr Thomas (Treasurer) Arthur Sutcliffe (Secretary). Front row, Arthur Brady, Robert Buchanan, John Espie, Peter Turnbull, Sandy Lang, Billy Bowes and James Hill.

Jimmy Ross record leading Burnley goalscorer in the 1897-98 with 23 goals scored and the first player to score 5 in a League game.

Fred Barron who on the 1st April 1911 against Barnsley made a record total of 400 League appearances

Team Photo. v West Bromwich Albion, Turf Moor 19th September 1908
Back row left to right.   (T H Holden Trainer), Hugh Moffatt, Jonathan Cretney,
Jerry Dawson, Alex Leake, Walter Abbott, Jonathan Parker,
Front row. Jonathan Morley, Fred Whittaker, Fred Barron, Richard Smith,
Arthur Bell, Albert Smith, William Howarth.

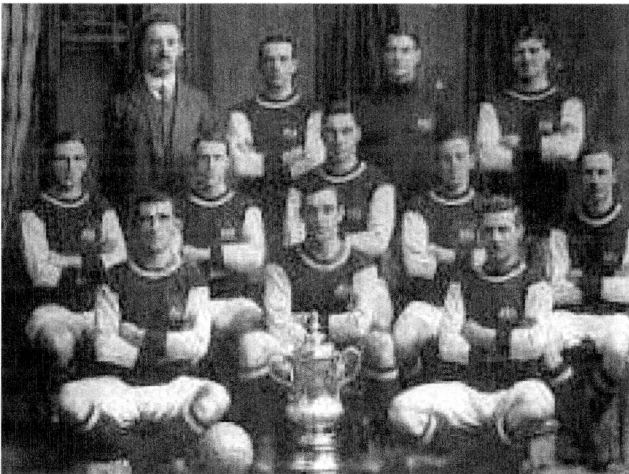

Burnley's 1914 FA Cup winning side.

Back row left to right (Ernest Edwards. Trainer). Tom Bamford, Ron Sewell,
David Taylor,
Middle row. Willie Nesbitt, Richard Lindley, Bert Freeman, Teddy Hodgson,
Eddie Mosscrop.
Front row. George Halley, Tommy Boyle, Willie Watson.

League champions 1920-21

Back row. Left to right. Alf Bassnett, Len Smelt, David Taylor, (Charlie Bates trainer). Jerry Dawson, Cliff Jones, Walter Weaver.
Middle row. Willie Nesbitt, Bob Kelly, Joe Anderson, Benny Cross, Eddie Mosscrop.
Front row. George Halley, Tommy Boyle, Willie Watson.

Burnley manager from 1910 to 1925. One promotion, one FA Cup win and one League Championship win.

104

Burnley line-up v Birmingham, 10th March 1926

Back row. Left to right. Benny Cross, Andy McCluggage, Tommy Hampson, (Charlie Bates trainer). Fred Blinkhorn, Louis Page, George Beel.
Front row. Jack Bruton, John Steel, Jack Hill, Harold Hargreaves, Billy Dougall, James Tonner.

Burnley line-up January 1932 v Wolverhampton Wanderers at Molineux.
Back row. Left to right. John Schofield, John Hall, Stan Bowsher, Richard Twist, Jim Brown, (Charlie Bates trainer) Tommy Willighan.
Front row. Sam Jennings, George Beel, Evan Jenkins, George Waterfield, Tom Jones , Louis Page

Burnley line up. 1946-47

Back row left to right. Reg Attwell. Arthur Woodruff, Jimmy Strong. Harold Mather. George Bray.
Front row. Jackie Chew, Billy Morris. Alan Brown. Ray Harrison Harry Potts, Peter Kippax.

Chairman Bob Lord and Harry Potts

League Championship side. 1959-60

Back row. Left to right. Alex Elder, Jimmy Robson, Tommy Cummings, Adam Blacklaw, Brian Miller, John Angus, Ray Pointer.
Front row. John Connelly. Jimmy McIlroy. Jimmy Adamson. Brian Pilkington, Trevor Meredith.

1960 Burnley players celebrating their success on team coach

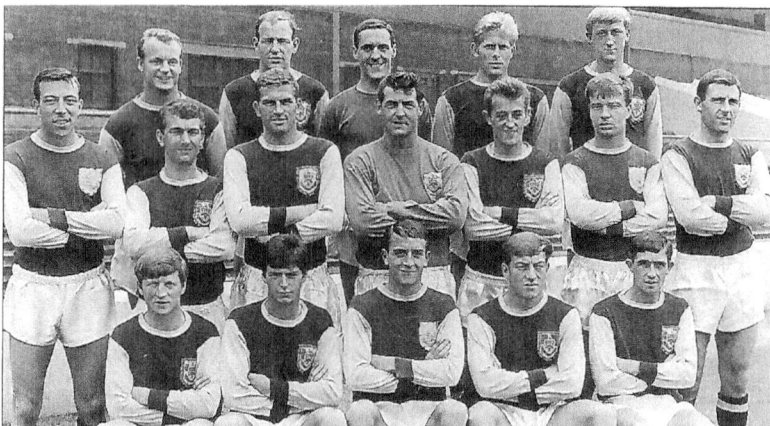

Burnley squad 1965

Back row left to right. Gordon Harris, Andy Lochhead, Harry Thomson, Ray Pointer, Sammy Todd,
Middle row. John Talbut, Brian O'Neil, Brian Miller, Adam Blacklaw, Arthur Bellamy, Alex Elder, John Angus,
Front row. Ian Towers, Willie Morgan, Willie Irvine, Ralph Coates, Freddie Smith.

Burnley team line Up. Second Division Champions 1972-73

Back row. Left to right. Jim Thomson, Colin Waldron, Alan Stevenson, Jeff Parton, Keith Newton.
Middle row. Mike Docherty, Doug Collins, Alan West, Geoff Nulty, Harry Wilson, Dave Thomas, Leighton James,
Front row. Billy Ingham, Frank Casper, Paul Fletcher, Martin Dobson, Eric Probert, Paul Bradshaw.

1981-82 Division Three winning side.

Back row. Left to right. Billy Hamilton, Alan Stevenson, David Holt, Billy O'Rourke, Paul Dixon, David Miller, Vince Overson, Lee Dixon, Andy Wharton, Steve Taylor, Billy Wright.
Front row. Mike Phelan, Derek Scott, Phil Cavener, Brian Laws, Trevor Steven, Paul McGee, Frank Casper (coach), Brian Miller (Manager) Martin Dobson. (Captain).

Ian Britton scoring against Orient in 1987

David Eyres and Gary Parkinson with 1994 play off trophy

1999-2000 Division Two promotion winning
goalscorer with 27 League goals scored. Andy Payton

Robbie Blake. Leading goalscorer in the
2003-04 and 2004-05 seasons

2009 Promotion winning squad

2016 Championship winning celebrations

Sean Dyche. Loyal servant for
9 and a half years

Tom Heaton Burnley England
international in May 2016, the first
since Martin Dobson in June 1974

Vincent Kompany. Burnley full time manager June 2022

ANSWERS AND FACTS

Quiz 1 Answers and Facts

1. **C.** Benny Green, in his first season at Burnley having been transferred from Birmingham in September of 1909 went on to become the leading goalscorer with 18 goals in the 1909–10 season and was Burnley's top goalscorer on another occasion before moving to Preston North End in May 1911.

2. **B.** Halley, Boyle and Watson first played together in the Second Division League fixture at Turf Moor on 15 March 1913 against Bury. They made their final appearances together in the home fixture against Blackburn Rovers on 11 February 1922 where they lost 1–2.

3. **B.** Burnley's Jack Hill became captain of England in the international at Turf Moor against Wales on 28 November 1927 which ended in a 1–2 defeat for England. He made eight international appearances whilst at Burnley before his transfer to Newcastle United in October 1928.

4. **A.** Steven Caldwell was the Burnley captain in the Championship Play Off Final in May 2009 against Sheffield United who they beat 1–0. Stephen went on to play for Wigan Athletic in May 2010.

5. **C.** Leading league goalscorer in 1956 Peter McKay was Scottish and was purchased from Dundee United in May 1954. He made a total of 66 senior appearances, scoring 38 goals before moving to St. Mirren in January 1957.

6. **A.** Leading league goalscorer Martin Paterson scored a total of 13 League goals in the 2008–09 season as well as a further six goals to make it a total of 19 for the season. He was purchased by manager Owen Coyle from Scunthorpe United for a fee of

£1.3 million. He was eventually transferred to Huddersfield Town .

7. **C.** Marlon Beresford in his three spells at Burnley made a total of 286 League appearances plus another 63 other senior appearances to bring his total at Burnley to 349. He eventually played for Bradford City .

8. **B.** Adrian Heath was Burnley's first player manager in the 1996–97 season. His first game in charge was at Wycombe Wanderers on 30 March 1996 when he was eventually subbed. He left the following season joining Everton in June 1997 as assistant to manager Howard Kendall.

9. **A.** Leading league goalscorer Gareth Taylor scored a total of 16 League goals in the 2001–02 season. He made a total of four international appearances for Wales whilst at Burnley before moving to Nottingham Forest in August 2003 having made a total of 106 senior appearances scoring a total of 37 goals.

10. **C.** Stephen Cotterill replaced Stan Ternent in the June of 2004. He did well for his previous club Cheltenham Town from the Southern League, then as Conference winners and FA Trophy winners as well as gaining League status for the club. He resigned as Burnley manager in October 2007 before moving on to Notts County. Portsmouth and Bristol City.

Quiz 2 Answers and Facts

1. **C.**   Joe Brown took over the managerial role at Burnley in January 1976 from Jimmy Adamson. Although his playing career was in the lower divisions, he arrived at Burnley in 1952 and made 6 League appearances, but due to injuries had to curtail his playing career. He became third team coach in 1961 and was later instrumental in Burnley's FA Youth Cup success in 1968 He was in the managers roll until the February of 1977.

2. **A.**   Ray Hankin and Peter Noble were joint league goalscorers in the 1975–76 relegation season. Peter Noble was also the leading league goalscorer the following season which was quite a feat for a half-back equalling his previous goal tally of 13.

3. **C.**   Tony Morley was the clubs record £100,000 signing in February 1976 and made his First Division league debut at Turf Moor against Ipswich Town. He had 2 spells at Burnley making a total of 107 senior appearances before returning to West Bromwich Albion in November 1988 following a loan spell.

4. **C.**   Burnley's new strip included a Blue V across the chest with a new badge with BFC in a circle. The new strip was used for a total of 4 seasons.

5. **A.**   Colin Waldron's final appearance for Burnley before joining Manchester United was in the First division fixture at Liverpool on 27 March 1976. In total, he made 356 senior appearances in his nine seasons at Burnley.

6. **A.**   Burnley made their 3,000th Football League appearance at Turf Moor on 16 October 1976 against Charlton Athletic which ended 4–4. Two Saturdays later at Plymouth Argyle, they

recorded their 1,500th away fixture and celebrated with a 1–0 win.

7. **C.** Burnley were beaten 0–1 by Blackpool in the FA Cup third round tie at Bloomfield Road on 3 January 1976. Blackpool were a Second division side and to date Burnley have never beaten them in this competition.

8. **A.** Burnley were relegated in the 1975–76 with a total of 28 points and it was the fifth time they had been relegated from the top division of English football.

9. **C.** Ray Hankin was transferred to Leeds United in September 1976 having been with Burnley as a junior since February 1973. He made in total 139 senior appearances and scored a total of 47 goals.

10. **B.** On Burnley's return to the second division, their first league opponents were Wolverhampton Wanderers on 21 August 1976 and they came away with a goalless draw. Wolverhampton Wanderers finished the season as champions of that division.

Quiz 3 Answers and Facts

1. **B.** Bert Freeman scored a total of 5 FA Cup goals in a total of 6 ties against Leeds City, Gainsborough Trinity, Middlesborough twice and Sunderland twice in the semi-final. His overall scoring record was 36.

2. **C.** Stan Bowsher was Burnley's first Welsh international when he was selected for the international at Wrexham against Northern Ireland on 2 February 1929 which ended 2–2. It was his only cap for Wales whilst at Burnley and he made a total of 85 senior appearances before moving on to Rochdale in March 1933.

3. **B.** Colin McDonald, who was still an amateur in the 1949–50 season, was on loan to Southern League Headington United. The club had only just become professional and were the first football club to have installed floodlights and would eventually change the name of the club to Oxford United before becoming a football League side in 1961 replacing liquidated Accrington Stanley.

4. **B.** Sunderland were Burnley's FA Cup semi-final opponents at Bramall Lane on 29 March 1913 with the tie having to be replayed following a goalless draw. The replay was at St Andrews 4 days later and ended in a 2–3 defeat.

5. **C.** Record goalscorer George Beel in his career at Burnley scored a total of 11 hat-tricks. His first was against West Ham United at Turf Moor on 17 November 1923. He continued scoring hat-tricks against Newcastle United twice, Bolton Wanderers, Tottenham Hotspur, Derby County, Sheffield United, Birmingham City, Portsmouth, Leeds United and

Wolverhampton Wanderers. He was unable to do so in the 21 FA Cup appearances he made.

6. **C.**   Liverpool were Burnley's first English opponents on foreign soil when they met in Milan in an exhibition match on 25 May 1922 with the score 1–0 to Burnley, courtesy of a Bob Kelly goal.

7. **C.**   The Burnley selection committee took over the managerial duties from Tom Bromilow who had joined Crystal Palace in May 1935. Their first duty was to change the club strip to White shirts and Black shorts with black trim and were in charge until May 1945 when they appointed their first manager in ten years with former England international Cliff Britton taking over the role.

8. **A.**   True. Burnley goalkeeper Jack Hillman was selected for England in the international at Sunderland on 18 February 1899 and was in fact the first English goalkeeper to concede a penalty in the 13–2 win over Ireland. It was to become his only appearances for England whilst at Burnley.

9. **A.**   David and Jonathon Walders became the club's first set of brothers to have played together in a league match on 3 September 1904 at Turf Moor against West Bromwich Albion which ended in a 1–4 defeat. They both came from Barrow in 1903 and 1904 and were transferred to Oldham Athletic in May 1906.

10. **A.**   On 27 February 1999. Burnley met Gillingham in the League Two fixture at Turf Moor and were beaten 0–5 with all the away sides goals scored by Bob Taylor. Gillingham that season were unlucky to have been beaten in the play-off final by Manchester City.

Quiz 4 Answers and Facts

1. **B.** Charlie Fletcher was transferred to Burnley from Brentford in February 1936 and in his 21-month stay made a total of 65 senior appearances, scoring a total of 22 goals before moving to Plymouth Argyle in October 1937. He was top League goalscorer in the 1936–37 season with 12 goals which was unique for a winger.

2. **A.** Burnley's first opponents to visit outside of Lancashire were Burslem Port Vale who they met on 12 October 1885 which was 5 days before Burnley met Darwen Old Wanderers in their first ever tie in the FA Cup where their second-choice team lost 0–11. Burnley lost the game at Vale 2–5 with no records of the scorers.

3. **C.** Burnley's first Scottish opponents were Glasgow side Cowlairs who visited Turf Moor on New Year's Day 1885 with the result 2–2 with Burnley scorers Arthurs and Strachan In the following two days, Kilmarnock and Glasgow Northern were the visitors with Burnley losing 2–3 to Kilmarnock but beat Glasgow Northern 4–0.

4. **C.** John Aird, who had been purchased from Perth junior side Jeanfield Swift's in August 1948, was to make a total of 143 senior appearances before emigrating to New Zealand in 1955. He became the clubs first Scottish international when he was selected for his national side against Norway at Hampden Park on 5 May 1954. He made a further three international appearances, against Norway two weeks later for a second time followed by Austria and Uruguay in the World Cup Finals in Switzerland in 1954.

5. **B.** Rotherham United were runners up to Burnley in the 1992 Division Four Championship season with 77 points to Burnley's

83. In the opening game of that season, Rotherham beat Burnley 1–2 at Millmoor and the result was repeated on Boxing Day by the same score at Turf Moor.

6. **C.** Burnley legend Bob Kelly was transferred to Sunderland in December 1925 for a record outgoing fee of £6,500. In his 12 years at the club, he made a club record 11 International appearances for England scoring 6 times. He was a member of the 1921 League championship winning side and made a total of 299 senior appearances scoring 97 goals.

7. **B.** Danny Ings was signed by ex AFC Bournemouth manager Eddie Howe, who had become Burnley manager in August 2011. Danny Ings became leading league goalscorer in 2014 and 2015 before moving to Liverpool in June 2015 where he won his first England international cap. He made a total of 122 senior appearances for Burnley scoring 38 goals.

8. **C.** Burnley, who were Second Division Champions in 1973, were selected to play First Division Manchester City at Maine Road on 18 August 1973 and beat them 1–0 thanks to a Colin Waldron header. It was the third time that Burnley had been involved in this Charity Shield event, having lost to Tottenham Hotspur 0–2 in 1921 and drawing 2–2 with Wolverhampton Wanderers in 1961.

9. **C.** In 1901 having played in red for the past 4 seasons the club changed to green shirts and white shorts. The strip was used for about 10 seasons before new Burnley manager John Haworth decided to change to the current strip of claret and blue that had been worn by Aston Villa.

10. **B.** Goalkeeper Tom Heaton was bestowed with the Burnley captaincy by manager Sean Dyche at the start of the 2015–16 and is thought to be the first time that a Burnley keeper had had the honour of leading his club. It is believed that former

keeper Jack Hillman may have had that honour but records are vague as to whether that is correct.

Quiz 5 Answers and Facts

1. **C.** Robbie Brady was purchased from Norwich City on 31 January 2017 for a then record purchase of £13 million. In his 4 seasons at Burnley, the Republic of Ireland player made a total of 81 senior appearances, scoring four goals before moving to AFC Bournemouth in 2021.

2. **A.** Paul Robinson, the former England goalkeeper, became the 90th keeper to have made a senior appearance for Burnley. In his two seasons At the club from 2015 to 2017 he made a total of three senior appearances

3. **A.** Burnley goalkeeper Tom Heaton was previously at Cardiff City until 2012 when he joined Bristol City where he made a total of 43 senior appearances before joining Burnley.

4. **C.** Five Burnley players were selected by their national side in the 2015–16 season. They were Scott Arfield who made three appearances for Canada, Danny Lafferty made one appearance for Northern Ireland, Stephen Ward six appearances for the Republic of Ireland, Sam Vokes 11 appearances for Wales and Tom Heaton for England who made his first international appearance against Australia .

5. **C.** In the final seven league fixtures of the 1894–95 season, Burnley lost them all, to Everton twice, Stoke twice, Small Heath, Aston Villa and Sunderland and they also went a total of nine games without a win.

6. **B.** The first League game to be televised live from Turf Moor was in the 1994–95 season when Burnley hosted Sheffield United on 20 November 1994 with the result a 4–2 win for Burnley that lifted them clear of the relegation zone of Division One.

7. **C.** When the Burnley manager John Bond resigned from his post at the beginning of the 1984–85 season, his assistant John Benson took over his duties. Burnley were relegated for the first time to the fourth tier of English football at the end of his first full season.

8. **C.** Leeds United were Burnley's first visitors to Turf Moor on 15 September 1974 when the new Brunshaw Road Stand was opened. The result was a 2–1 victory for Burnley. The stand was subsequently named the Bob Lord Stand at a later date after it was thought appropriate in honour of the chairman.

9. **C.** Jimmy Adamson had the honour of becoming the footballer of the year in the 1961–62 season with his side Burnley having been runners up in both the League and FA Cup that season. Apparently the runner up position went to Burnley's Jimmy McIlroy.

10. **A** Leading league goalscorer Ray Pointer scored a total of 25 goals in the 1961–62 season. He was also top scorer with 27 in the 1958–59 season and in his 8 seasons at Burnley made a total of 270 senior appearances scoring 132 goals in total.

Quiz 6 Answers and Facts

1. **A.** Bob Kelly and Jerry Dawson were the first two Burnley players to play together for England at Villa Park on 8 April 1922 against Scotland. The game ended in a 0–1 defeat for England. It was Dawson's first cap and Kelly's sixth and would be the only time that they would play together for England.

2. **C.** Bob Kelly became the most capped Burnley player for England and would play a total of 11 internationals , his first was against Scotland on 10 April 1920 at Hillsborough where he scored two goals. His final appearance for England as a Burnley player was on 4 April 1925 against Scotland and he scored a total of six goals in his 11 appearances before making another three appearances and scoring a further two goals whilst at his next league club.

3. **C** Leading Burnley goalscorer Harry Potts was transferred to Everton in October 1950 for a record outgoing fee of £20,000 having been at Burnley, firstly as a junior in 1937. He made a total of 181 senior appearances scoring 50 goals as well as being leading League goalscorer on three occasions. It would not be the last time that Harry Potts would be associated with the club and would in future bring success as a very astute Football manager at the club that would span a total of nearly of fifteen years in two periods with the 1960 League Championship win of 1960 his proudest achievement

4 **C.** It was Eintracht Frankfurt who finally eliminated Burnley from the 1966–67 Inter-Cities Fairs Cup in the 4th round having eliminated VfB Stuttgart, Lausanne-Sports and Napoli in the previous rounds. In the two-legged 4th round tie, Burnley in

the 1st leg held Eintracht Frankfurt 1–1 in Germany but lost in the home tie at Turf Moor 1–2 to finally exit the competition.

5. **A.** Burnley in the Second division promotion season of 1946–47 under manager Cliff Britton conceded just 29 goals partly due to the goalkeeping skills of Jimmy Strong who himself broke records that season and would eventually make a record number of consecutive appearances.

6. **C.** Andy Payton scored a total of 27 League goals in the 1999–2000 Division Two promotion winning season , the highest since 1966 He was leading league goalscorer at Burnley on three consecutive seasons and in his five years at the club made 131 plus appearances scoring a total of 81 goals .

7. **A.** Jack Butterfield was the only player to make his debut for Burnley in 1947–48 season when he made the right back position in the First division fixture at Charlton Athletic on 20 September 1947. He made two other League appearances that eason before becoming a scout at the Club in 1949.

8. **B.** Billy Hamilton scored a total of 11 goals for Burnley in the Division Three championship season of 1981–82. The Northern Ireland international became leading league goalscorer Burnley on three other occasions and in his five seasons at the club made 251 senior appearances scoring a total of 77 goals before his transfer to Oxford United in 1984.

9. **A.** Bert Freeman scored a total of 31 goals in the promotion winning season of 1912–13 and was one less than his club record breaking 32 of the previous season. He was to spend a total of 10 seasons at Burnley making a total of 189 senior appearances, scoring a total of 115 goals as well as three international appearances for England before finally joining Wigan Borough in 1921.

10. **A.** In the first round of the FA Cup at Turf Moor on 17 January 1891 Burnley played Crewe Alexander and at the end of 90 minutes, the score was 1–1. Instead of playing the replayed tie at Crewe, an extra 30 minutes was added with Alex McLardie scoring the winning goal in the 115th minute to earn a place in the following round at Notts County where Burnley lost 1–2.

Quiz 7 Answers and Facts

1. **A.** Jimmy Ross, who was one of the Preston North End's Invincibles of the 1888–89 season, came to Burnley in March 1897 from Liverpool and was instrumental in Burnley's 1898 promotion campaign. In the replayed FA Cup first round tie at Sheffield United, Jimmy Ross scored from the penalty spot in the 22nd minute but it was not enough as Burnley were eliminated from the competition 1–2 with United going on to win that season's competition beating Derby County in the Final. Two days later, he made his final appearance for Burnley at Newcastle United before moving to Manchester City having played a total of 63 senior games and scoring 33 goals.

2. **A.** John Talbut was the first Burnley player to have scored a penalty for the club in the Football League Cup replay at Turf Moor on 29 September 1966 against Shrewsbury Town in a second round replay . The final score was 5–0 to Burnley with John scoring from the spot in the 10th minute. Burnley were beaten 0–2 at Sheffield United in the following round.

3. **C.** Controversial Burnley chairman Bob Lord started his career as a butcher eventually selling door to door. He eventually owned a string of butcher shops throughout the town. He became chairman in June 1955 and finally retired from his post in October 1981.

4. **C.** Richard Chaplow was originally a trainee at the club from September 2003. Having started a total of 56 games plus 18 games as substitute scoring seven goals, he was transferred to Premier League side West Bromwich Albion for a record outgoing fee of £1.5 million.

5. **B.** Burnley became a professional football club in 1883 following a lot of disagreements with other clubs and authorities and felt the the only way forward to entice the many Scottish players that came to the club was to become professional. The FA Cup rules remained the same with only amateurs from their own town taking part.

6. **B.** Steven Fletcher broke two records at Burnley when firstly transferred from Hibernian for a record £3 million fee in June 2009. He stayed at Premier league club Burnley for one season having made a total of 35 senior appearances and scoring eight goals. He was transferred to Wolverhampton Wanderers for £6.5 million which was a record outgoing fee in June 2010.

7. **C.** Maxwel Cornet before becoming an Ivory Coast full international played for France at under 21 level. He played at all the levels from under 16s to the under 21s making a total of 52 appearances and scoring 24 goals. In 2017 he decided to play for the Ivory Coast as a full international and up to April 2022 has played a total of 29 internationals scoring six times.

8. **B.** Ten Burnley players made appearances for their nations in the 2016 season which included Scott Arfield for Canada, Jeff Hendrick for Northern Ireland, Robbie Brady, Stephen Ward and Kevin Long for the Republic of Ireland, Michael Keane and Tom Heaton for England, Sam Vokes for Wales, Johann Gudmundsson for Iceland and Steven Defour for Belgium.

9. **A.** On Tuesday 8 February 2022 Burnley celebrated their 5,000th league game against Manchester United at Turf Moor. The very first game was on 8 September 1888 against Preston North End at Deepdale where they lost 2–5 The score in the 5,000th League fixture was 1–1, with a Jay Rodriguez equaliser.

10. **C.** Burnley manager Sean Dyche was in his position for a total of 9 years and 6 months before being dismissed on 15 April 2022. He had remarkable success having kept the club in the Premier league of English football for seven seasons and lifting them to promotion twice. He was the third longest Burnley manager behind Harry Potts and John Haworth and probably in the top three of all the Burnley managers in the club's history.

Quiz 8 Answers and Facts

1. **C.** Burnley goalkeeper Colin McDonald was first selected for the first division fixture at Aston Villa on 10 April 1954 and the result was a 1–5 defeat. He however was selected for the final four fixtures conceding four goals. He became the club's regular keeper as well as England's first choice making a total of eight international appearances. Owing to a serious injury playing for the Football League, he was forced to retire in 1961 having played a total of 201 senior games.

2. **C.** Lincoln City were the unfortunate club to be automatically relegated from the Fourth Division in 1987 to play non-league football, and were promoted back the following season. Thanks to Burnley's 2–1 win over Orient in the final game of the season, the club survived by one point to guarantee Football League football for a further season.

3. **B.** Robbie Brady Burnley's record purchase from Norwich City in January 2017 was previously with Hull City before he joined the Canaries. In his four seasons at Burnley, the Republic of Ireland international played a total of 81 senior appearances before moving to AFC Bournemouth in 2021.

4. **C.** Burnley and Northern Ireland full-back Alex Elder joined Stoke City in August 1967 having played a total of 330 senior games as well as being selected for his country 34 times. He became club captain as well as being involved in the club's 1960 League championship win and an FA Cup appearance in 1962.

5. **C.** Billy Elliott scored two goals for England in the international At Wembley on 26 November 1952 against Belgium. He was capped for England a total of five times before joining Sunderland in June 1953 for a record outgoing fee. In his two

full seasons at the club, he made a total of 82 senior appearances scoring 16 goals.

6. **A.** Jimmy McIlroy, who was to become the club's most capped player scored a total of 10 goals for Northern Ireland whilst at Burnley and made 51 international appearances. He made a further four appearances for Northern Ireland after he was transferred to Stoke City in March 1963.

7. **C.** Both Ray Pointer and John Connelly scored for England in the International at Wembley against Portugal on 25 October 1961. It was to be Ray Pointers final appearance for England with John Connelly making a further four international appearances before being transferred to Manchester United where he was selected a further 10 times.

8. **C.** Burnley's non-league opponents in the third round of the FA Cup on 5 January 2002 we're Essex sixth tier side Canvey Island who had already beaten Wigan Athletic and Northampton Town in the previous rounds, Burnley beat Canvey Island at Turf Moor 4–1 with record signing Ian Moore getting his first hat-trick at the club.

9 **B.** The first FA Cup tie following World War Two was the two-legged tie against Stoke City .The first leg of the tie was at Stoke on 5 January 1946 where they were defeated 1–3. In the second leg third round tie at Turf Moor on 7 January 1946, Burnley were the 2–1 victors but were eliminated 3–4 on Aggregate. A total of 13 players were used.

10. **A.** Arthur Woodruff was indeed the second oldest player to play for Burnley and made his final appearance at Chelsea on 19 April 1952 at the age of 39 years 7 days. In his 16 years' service, he made a total of 292 senior appearances.

Quiz 9 Answers and Facts

1. **B.** Louis Page was leading league goalscorer twice in the 1925–26 season with 26 and in the 1929–30 season with 15. He will be remembered for the six goals he scored at Birmingham in April 1926 where Burnley beat their rivals 7–1 to secure first division football for another season.

2. **A.** The first player to score a hat-trick on his League debut was Tom Nicol at Turf Moor on 7 March 1891 against Preston North End. He was signed from Scottish junior side Mossend Swift's in February 1891 and in his five seasons became leading goalscorer twice and made a total of 149 senior appearances scoring 44 goals.

3. **C.** Andy Payton became the first Burnley player to score a hat-trick as a substitute at Turf Moor on 22 August 2000 against Hartlepool United in the first round, first leg of the Football League Cup. The final score was 4–1 to Burnley who lost 2–3 in the second leg but got through to the next round 6-4 on aggregate.

4. **C.** Record £1 million purchase Ian Moore came to Burnley from Stockport County in November 2000. In his four plus years at Burnley played a total of 193 plus senior games scoring 50 goals before joining Leeds United in March 2005 for a £50,000 fee, His father Ronnie Moore was manager at the time of Tranmere Rovers.

5. **A.** Eric Probert became Burnley's top league goalscorer with five in the 1970–71 season, the lowest since the 1889–90 season when Robert Haresnape scored six. In total, Burnley in that 1970–71 relegation season scored a total of 29 goals, the lowest in the Clubs history.

6. **B.** Goalkeeper Jerry Dawson made a record 522 league appearances . His first was in the division Two fixture at Turf Moor on 13 April 1907 against Stockport County, his only appearance that season. keeping a clean sheet in the clubs 3–0 victory. His final appearance was at Turf Moor on Christmas Day 1928 against Liverpool where Burnley won 3–2 making it a total of 20 years eight months as a player at the club.

7. **B.** Burnley at the beginning of the 1920–21 league championship season lost their first three league fixtures. From 6 September 1920 till 25 March 1921 they remained unbeaten in a total of 30 league games which at the time was a division one record. It was Manchester City who broke that record two days later beating the turfites 3–0.

8. **A.** Ian Towers became the club's first substitute when he replaced an injured Willie Irvine at Highbury against Arsenal on 28 August 1965 at the beginning of the second half when Burnley were leading 2–1.The full-time result ended 2–2.

9. **C.** In the history of Burnley Football Club where over 5,000 senior games had been played up until the end of the 2021–22 season, no goalkeeper has ever scored although Jerry Dawson came close when missing a penalty in a league game.

10. **C.** Joey Gudjonsson was the first substitute to come on for Burnley in the 27th minute replacing Chris McCann in the 2008–09 Play-off Final at Wembley. Burnley went on to win with a Wade Elliott goal in the first half securing Premier League football for the coming 2009–10 season.

Quiz10 Answers and Facts

1. **A.**   In the 1929–30 relegation season, Everton were bottom club with 35 points with Burnley above them on 36 points and Sheffield United also on 36 points but were relegated on goal average with Sheffield United on -1.5 and Burnley on -1.22. Everton were the Second Division Champions the following season with Burnley finishing in eighth position.

2. **A.**   The new cricket field stand was opened in 1969 replacing the old terracing, which was erected on railway sleepers, It was opened when Middlesbrough came to Burnley for a pre-season friendly in August 1969 and construction took up all of the previous season. Immediately after, Burnley demolished the Old Brunshaw Road stand which would later become the Bob Lord Stand.

3. **C.**   Prior to Johann Gudmundsson's selection for Iceland in the 1918 World Cup Finals in Russia, the previous player to have played in the Finals was Billy Hamilton for Northern Ireland in Spain who played a total of 5 games scoring twice against Austria in Madrid on 11 July 1982.

4 **C.**   Six players including Johann Gudmundsson have represented their countries in the World Cup Finals. The first was John Aird for Scotland in Switzerland in 1954 where he played twice. On 8 June 1958 both Jimmy McIlroy Northern Ireland and Colin McDonald England played in the finals in Sweden. Billy Hamilton was the fourth player from Burnley when he represented Northern Ireland in Spain in the 1982 finals and was followed by the inclusion of Tommy Cassidy with both of them playing together against hosts Spain in Valencia on 25 June 1982.

5 **B.**   Only two goals have been scored by a Burnley player in the World Cup Finals with Billy Hamilton scoring twice in the same

match for Northern Ireland against Austria in Madrid on 11 July 1982.

6. **C.** Burnley last played Aberdeen in a friendly at Turf Moor on 26 April 1930 and the score was 9–5 to Burnley. The goalscorers for the Turfites were Prest (2). Storer, McCluggage (pen.) Wallace ,Page, Pemberton, O'Dowd and Steel. Burnley who were already relegated beat Derby County 6–2 a week later at Turf Moor.

7. **C.** Goalkeeper Adam Blacklaw, who was from Aberdeen, attracted interest from several clubs including Aberdeen, his local club. Burnley signed him as a junior in October 1954 and he would eventually become Colin McDonald's replacement. He would eventually play for Burnley in all competitions making a total of 383 senior appearances before joining Blackburn Rovers in 1967.

8. **A.** Dougie Newlands signed for Burnley from Aberdeen in March 1955 and went on to make a total of 104 senior appearances scoring 23 goals before moving to Stoke City in July 1959.

9. **B.** Frank Hill became the clubs first Scottish manager when he took over from Cliff Britton in October 1948. He was a well-established former Arsenal player and won numerous honours with the gunners in the nineteen thirty's. He left Burnley in August 1954 to manage Preston North End and in his six years at Turf Moor established the club as a top first division side.

10. **B.** The second Scottish club to have played at Turf Moor were Kilmarnock on 2 January 1885 losing 2–3 having the previous day entertained Cowlairs who were based in Glasgow, the match ending 2–2.The following day Glasgow Northern became the third side to play at Turf Moor with Burnley beating them 4–0.

Quiz 11 Answers and Facts

1. **B.**   In the 1891–92 season, changes were made to the rules of football with goal nets introduced, referees instead of umpires and penalty kicks allowed for infringement. The first Burnley goalkeeper to save a penalty was Jack Hillman at Sunderland on 21 November, having also being the first to concede a penalty earlier in the same game.

2. **C.**   The record aggregate of 15–2 was recorded from both League fixtures against Darwen with them finishing bottom of the League in their first and only season of Division One football with a total of 112 goals conceded from 26 games.

3. **C.**   When Burnley played at Darwen on 2 April 1892, they at the time recorded their biggest away victory with a 6–2 win. The scorers for Burnley were Nicol (2) McLardie (2). Bowes and Hill.

4. **C.**   Jay Rodriguez's father Kiko was of Spanish descent and did in fact play for Burnley's reserve team. He mostly throughout his career played non-League football passing on his knowledge to his son Jay who would make over 200 senior appearances for Burnley as well as being selected for England.

5. **A.**   On 10 April 1892, Burnley, for the first time, played a League game in Manchester against Newton Heath (now Manchester United) and drew 1–1 with William Boyd scoring the opening goal for Burnley in the 60th minute.

6. **C.**   Andy Payton, who was born near Burnley and once turned down by the club, joined Scottish club Celtic and played in the 1992–93 season with 36 senior appearances scoring 15 goals before moving to Barnsley and Huddersfield Town and finally signed for Burnley in January 1998.

7. **C.** Albert Cheesebrough, Colin McDonald, Dougie Winton, Dougie Newlands and Les. Shannon all made their final appearances in the 1958–59 season, Colin McDonald's career was ended by an injury playing for the Football League with all the other players moved to other clubs

8. **C.** Bobby Seith who made 27 League appearances in the Championship winning season made his final appearance for Burnley at Sheffield Wednesday on 2 April 1960. In the August of 1960 he moved to Dundee where in his five seasons he made 134 senior appearances.

9. **C.** In the 1960–61 season, Burnley scored a total of 102 League goals. In the League game at Birmingham City on 27 April 1961, Burnley were awarded a penalty with Jimmy Adamson scoring from the spot to make it the clubs 100th League goal that season.

10. **B.** Jimmy Robson equalised for Burnley in the second half of play in 49th minute of the 1961–62 FA Cup Final making it the 100th goal to be scored in a Wembley final. Tottenham Hotspur added a further two goals to claim the prize for the second successive season.

Quiz 12 Answers and Facts

1 **B.** In Burnley's opening League fixture against Colchester United at Turf Moor on 15 August 1987, there were seven team changes with only four players from the Orient game playing. They were defender Peter Leabrook, and midfielder and captain Ray Deakin. Forwards were the two previous goalscoring heroes in the previous game, Neil Grewcock and Ian Britton.

2. **C.** In the FA Cup First round tie at Astley Bridge on 23 October 1886. only Walter Place Junior was recorded as scoring two goals for Burnley In the 3–3 drawn tie. The other scorer was recorded as unknown with the replay at Turf Moor seven days later resulting in another 2–2 drawn tie with Jack Keenan recorded as scorer of the second goal. Both clubs decided to withdraw from that season's competition.

3. **C.** Burnley have played at Wembley Stadium a total of seven times. The first was in the 1947 Cup Final against Charlton Athletic and the second was against Tottenham Hotspur in the 1962 Cup Final, losing on both occasions. In the 1988 Football League Trophy Final at Wembley Burnley made their third visit where they lost to Wolverhampton Wanderers. In 1994, they won for the first time beating Stockport County in the Division Two Play-off Final. Their fifth visit was the Championship Play-off final in 2009 where they beat Sheffield United 1–0 to be promoted back to the top tier of English football for the first time since 1976. Two League fixtures were played against Tottenham Hotspur at Wembley Stadium in the 2017–18 and 2018–19 season due to the construction of Tottenham's new stadium. The record for the seven visits is Won 2. Drawn 1. Lost 4.

4. **C.** When Joe Hart came to Burnley in July 2018, he came to the club as the most capped goalkeeper having made a total of 75 appearances for England. When Gabor Kiraly came to Burnley in 2007, he was then the most capped international keeper having made a total at the time if 69 appearances for Hungary. His final total stands at 108 appearances and was the oldest ever player to have participated in the Euro Championships in 2016. Tony Waiters made five goalkeeping appearances for England.

5. **B.** Since the 1935–36 season, the club strip was White shirts and Black shorts which they wore throughout the 1945–46 campaign with just two senior games played, then of the FA Cup third round two-legged tie against Stoke City in January 1946. For the start of the 1946–47 season, with new manager Cliff Britton in charge, the club colours changed back to claret and blue as requested by the many supporters.

6. **B.** The inscription on each of the medals read. English Cup Winners and not FA Cup Winners. They were presented to the Burnley team at the Old Crystal Palace stadium by the first monarch to attend a final. King George V on 25 April 1914.

7. **C.** At the beginning of the 1934–35 season. They opened the season with a home League fixture against Southampton and wore Blue Shirts with claret sleeves. The strip was used for one season before changing to White shirts and Black shorts .

8. **A.** In 1882, Blackburn Rovers played Accrington at Turf Moor in the final of the Lancashire Senior cup with the result a 3–1 win for the Rovers. It was a good eight months before Burnley moved to Turf Moor in the February of 1983 where they were beaten 3–6 by Rawtenstall.

9. **C.** The only player to make his League debut for Burnley in the 1965–66 Season was Len Kinsella when he came on as substitute replacing right back John Angus in the League fixture at Turf Moor on 20 November 1965. He made a further three games as substitute that season and only made seven full appearances and seven substitutions throughout his career at Burnley before moving to Carlisle United in 1970.

10. **A.** William Smith became the clubs first goalkeeper to have played in a League game when he conceded five goals at Preston North End. He played a further two League games before being replaced by Robert Kaye who went on to make five appearances. Forward Fred Poland was selected for the first League encounter against Blackburn Rovers and conceded seven before a Mr W. Cox took over for the remaining 13 fixtures.

Quiz 13 Answers and Facts

1. **C.** William Lambie was an imposter who duped Burnley into signing him, claiming that he was a junior Scottish international who played for both Clyde and Queens Park and was a prolific goalscorer. He was selected for the second division game at Turf Moor on 19 October 1901 against Burton United which ended goalless. His first half performance was very poor to say the least with Burnley having to remove him from the field of play. From then on there has never been any trace of him or his whereabouts.

2. **B.** Bert Freeman in his England international selections whilst at Burnley played a total of three games. The first was on 10 February 1912 in Dublin against Ireland where he scored in England's 6–1 victory. The second was at Wrexham against Wales on 11 March 1912 where he scored his second. The final international was at Hampden Park on 23 March 1912 against Scotland which ended 1–1 and his total was two goals from three Internationals played.

3. **C.** Burnley in the 1999–2000 Division Two promotion season made a total of 88 points. Preston North End the eventual champions were on 95 with Burnley clear of third placed Gillingham on 85. It was only at the closing stages that Burnley become eventual promotion challengers with the likes of Ian Wright and Andy Payton who scored a total of 27 League goals.

4. **B.** Burnley's first £1 million purchase Ian Moore, having played a total of 193 plus appearances scoring 50 goals was transferred to Leeds United in March 2005.

5. **A.** The leading league goalscorer for Burnley in the 2002–03 season was Gareth Taylor who was also the seasons previous

top scorer In his 2-year-6-month stay, the Welsh international played a total of 98 plus senior appearances scoring a total of 37 goals before moving to Nottingham Forest.

6. **C.** Goalkeeper Peter Mellor was an apprentice at Manchester City before moving to non-league Witton Albion for two seasons. He attracted the attentions of Burnley who gave him a trial. He was selected for the opening league fixture at Derby County and suffered a hand injury. After his two years six month stay with the Clarets he joined Fulham where in the 1975 Cup Final he was on the losing side beaten by West Ham United.

7. **A.** Due to the treacherous weather conditions in the January of 1947 as well as the many FA Cup ties that Burnley had to play the season overran with the club having to play their first ever fixture on 7 June 1947 at Millwall where the result for the already promoted Burnley ended 1–1.

8. **A.** Paul Barnes was the last Burnley player to have scored five goals in a league fixture. It happened at Turf Moor on 5 October 1996 against Stockport County. His final goal in the fixture was in the 78th minute and he was subsequently subbed and maybe could have bettered or beaten Louis Pages record at Birmingham in 1926 of six goals scored.

9. **B.** Burnley played a total of nine FA Cup ties including the Final against Charlton Athletic in 1947, On the way to Wembley, they beat Aston Villa 5–1, Coventry City 2–0, Luton Town 3–0 after a goalless draw, Middlesbrough 1–0 after a 2–2 draw and Liverpool in the semi-final beating them 1–0 following a goalless draw.

10. **B.** Six players made their League debuts for Burnley following World War Two at the start of the 1946–47 season. They were goalkeeper Jimmy Strong, full back Harry Mather, half back

Harry Spencer, wingers Jackie Chew and Frank Kippax and inside forward Harry Potts.

Quiz 14 Answers and Facts

1. **C.** Accrington like Burnley were original members of the Football League but were not the same club as today, they originally amalgamated and took the name Stanley from a name of a public house. The last Burnley player to score against Accrington was Robert Buchanan at Accrington on 14 January 1893.

2. **A.** Burnley goalkeeper Colin McDonald who made eight appearances for England conceded a total of 11 goals. His first game was a friendly against the USSR in Moscow on 18 May 1958 which ended a goal apiece. He was selected for the four World Cup final games in Sweden 1958 where he conceded a total of five goals against Brazil, Austria and the USSR twice. He played a further three internationals against Northern Ireland USSR and Wales where he conceded a further total of five goals. Colin McDonalds international career came to a tragic end having been seriously injured playing for the Football League in Ireland.

3. **C.** Robbie Blake was the leading League goalscorer in the 2004–05 season with 10 and these were scored up to and including his last game for Burnley first time round at Sunderland on 18 December 2004. A total of 17 goals were scored by Burnley out of the remaining 22 games left to play. He was sorely missed following his move to Birmingham City.

4. **A** Lucas Jutkiewicz was purchased from Middlesbrough by Burnley manager Sean Dyche in August 2014 and played a total of 32 senior games without scoring once. He was subsequently loaned to Bolton Wanderers and then Birmingham City where

he scored a total of 15 goals before joining City on a permanent basis.

5. **A.** Goalkeeper Paul Robinson came to Burnley as back up to Tom Heaton from Blackburn Rovers and in his England international career made 41 appearances. He throughout the 2016–17 season at Burnley made three appearances before finally retiring.

6. **A.** Edward Heath was the former Conservative Prime Minister who open the new Brunshaw Road stand on 14th September 1974 for the fixture against Leeds United

7. **A.** True. Burnley goalkeeper Tom Heaton was in fact the 110th goalkeeper to represent England when he came on to the field of play in the 87th minute in a friendly at the Stadium of Light Sunderland on the 27 May 2016. He was the first Burnley player since Martin Dobson in 1974 to represent England.

8. **C.** Burnley manager Stan Ternent gave a total of 21 players their senior debuts for Burnley. Nineteen of these players were given League debuts. The following season, eight of these players remained and were instrumental in the club's push for promotion finally finishing as Division Two runners up to Preston North End.

9. **B.** It was Gordon Harris who replaced Brian Pilkington in the number 11 shirt and made his debut in the 1958–59 season. Brian Pilkington made his final appearance for Burnley at Turf Moor against Sheffield Wednesday on 11 February 1961, before moving to Bolton Wanderers the following month with Gordon Harris now the permanent left winger for Burnley.

10. **A.** Gifton Noel Williams became the first Burnley player to come on as substitute and score a hat-trick in a league match. It was on 12 September 2006 at Turf Moor against Barnsley when he replaced midfielder Alan Mahon in the 34th minute and scored his goals in the second half in the 57th , 83rd and 90th minute

Quiz 15 Answers and Facts

1. **C.** There were eight Burnley players who played prior to World War Two and after. They were full-backs Arthur Woodruff and Jack Marshall. Half-back George Bray and forwards Jack Billingham , Billy Morris , Jack Knight , Ron Hornby and Fred Taylor.

2. **A.** First Division Burnley suffered one of the biggest shock defeats in their entire history when they were beaten at Turf Moor in the third round of the FA Cup on 4 January 1975 by Southern League Wimbledon 0–1. The talk prior to the tie was how many goals would Burnley beat them by! Wimbledon would eventually play in the top division of English football as well as winning the FA cup competition with Burnley languishing in the fourth tier.

3. **C.** Burnley's Martin Dobson was selected for England four times in the 1973–74 season. His first was on 3 April 1974 in Lisbon against Portugal which ended goalless. On 29 May 1974 in Leipzig he played against East Germany which ended 1–1 with another cap three days later in Sofia against Bulgaria which ended 1–0 to England. His fourth and final cap as a Burnley player was in Belgrade against Yugoslavia on 5 June 1974 which ended 2–2.

4 **A.** Derby County paid £310,000 for Leighton James in November 1975 Which was a club outgoing record. In September 1978, he returned to Burnley for a second time having been purchased from Queens Park Rangers for a £165,000 fee and Stayed for two seasons before moving to Swansea City for a £130,000 fee. He would return for a third time in July 1986 from Newport County in 1886 and would be in the team that played in the

relegation battle against the Orient in 1987. He made a total of 393 plus senior appearances before being released in May 1989 having also scored a total of 81 goals.

5. **C.**   Burnley goalscoring legend Ray Pointer returned to the club as a youth team coach in 1978 having played for Bury, Coventry City, Portsmouth and finally non-league Waterlooville. In his eight seasons at Burnley made 270 senior appearances scoring 132 goals and was also capped for England three times, whilst at the club scoring twice in 1961.

6. **A.**   Martin Dobson returned to Burnley in August 1979 from Everton and stayed for five seasons before moving to Bury in March 1984. In his twelve seasons at Burnley he played a total of 493 plus senior games scoring a total of 76 goals.

7. **B.**   Brian Miller returned to Burnley as manager in July 1986 having been in that position from October 1979 to January 1983. He was in charge of the side that played the Orient on 9 May 1987 and was instrumental in keeping the club in the Football League. A season later, he led them out at Wembley in the final of the Football League Trophy where they lost to Wolverhampton Wanderers 0–2. He stayed in his position until January 1989 before embarking on a new role within the club of chief scout. In his footballing career he made a total of 455 senior appearances scoring 37 goals in his thirteen seasons at the club.

8. **B.**   The 1986–87 season was summed up for Burnley when Hereford United came to Turf Moor on 24 January 1987 and beat them 0–6 dropping them firmly amongst the fourth division. relegation candidates .In the following seasons fixture. Burnley managed a goalless draw against the previous seasons victors.

9. **B.** Five goalkeepers were used in the Division Four championship season. Chris Pearce made 14 appearances followed by Andy Marriott with 15 appearances. Dave Williams made 5, Nicol Walker made 6 and Mark Kendall made 2 appearances.

10. **A.** Defender Ben Mee came to Burnley in July 2011 on loan from Manchester City. He made his League debut against Watford at Turf Moor on 6 August which resulted in a 1–1 draw. A few years later, he was purchased for an undisclosed fee and up to the end of the 2020–21 season has made a total of 352 senior appearances scoring nine goals. He has been team captain since the 2017–18 season replacing goalkeeper Tom Heaton who was transferred to Aston Villa.

Quiz 16 Answers and Facts

1. **A.** In the opening league game at Turf Moor on 5 September 1914 against Bradford City, three changes were made with regular goalkeeper Jerry Dawson back in the side. Skipper Tommy Boyle was replaced in the centre-half position by Levy Thorpe and in the outside-left position was Reuben Grice who was purchased from Rotherham County and would make just two League appearances in his one season at the club. It was a fact that the winning team of 1914 never played together again.

2. **C.** In the 1902–03 season. Burnley Belvedere did in fact play their games at Turf Moor and were classed as Burnley reserves, Two players made debuts for Burnley with Cuthbert Storey and Arthur Bell who remained an amateur throughout his career. In his seven years at the club. Bell played a total of 104 senior games scoring 29 goals and was selected twice for England Amateurs.

3. **C.** Northern Ireland international Billy Hamilton came to Burnley from Queens Park Rangers in November 1979. He was leading League goalscorer four times in the 1979–80 season with 7, the 1981–82 season with 11, the 1982–83 season with 13 and the 1983–84 season with 18. He made a total of 251 senior appearances for Burnley scoring a total of 77 goals. He made a total of 34 international appearances scoring 5 goals.

4. **C.** The half-back Line up in the 1900–01 season read Barron, Bannister and Taylor and would be unchanged throughout the season. Fred Barron would go on to make a then record of 423 senior appearances in his 13 years at the Club. Billy Bannister would make a total of 58 senior appearances before moving to Bolton Wanderers in November 1901 as well as becoming the third player to be selected for England. Joe Taylor joined

Burnley in November 1893 and in his 14 years of loyal service would make a total of 352 senior appearances.

5. **A.** The first brothers to play together for Burnley were Jack and William Gair, who in the 1883–84 season which was not in League football as the honour goes to David and Jonathan Walders in the 1904–05 season. In the home game on 3 November 1979 against Orient, brothers Viv and Richard Overson became the second set of brothers to play together in a League game.

6. **C.** Goalkeeper Alan Stevenson was transferred to Burnley from Chesterfield in January 1972 and made his League debut at Orient on 22 January 1972 and would make a total of 540 senior appearances in his eleven years at the club.

7. **C.** Goalscoring legend George Beel came to Burnley from Chesterfield in April 1923 and would become the clubs highest goal scorer in the 1927–28 season with 35. He was leading League goalscorer six times with 11 hat-tricks from 11 years of loyal service. He scored a total of 179 goals from 337 senior appearances before moving to Lincoln City then finally to Rochdale.

8. **C.** When Burnley player Hugh Moffat, missed his train connection at Manchester Train station, he was too late for the game to be played that afternoon at Chesterfield on 26 November 1904.He did arrive for the Division Two game when it was finally over with the result of the game goalless.

9. **A.** Gainsborough Trinity were Burnley's second round FA Cup opponents at Turf Moor on 1 February 1913 where the visitors lost 1–4. The club were impressed with the full-backs, Sam Gunton and Cliff Jones as well as goalkeeper Ron Sewell that they signed all three, two hours after the game. Ron Sewell and

Cliff Jones would eventually become involved in the club's future successes.

10. **C.** Billy Ingham who joined Burnley as an apprentice in 1969 was substitute in a total of 30 League games as well as being sub in three further cup ties as a half-back. Throughout his 11 years at the club he made a total of 233 full appearances before moving to Bradford City in 1980.

Quiz 17 Answers and Facts

FA Cup 1914. Quiz

1. **B.** Bert Freeman had the honour of scoring the winning goal in the 1913–14 FA Cup Final. He came to Burnley as the all-time record goalscorer at Everton and was purchased with a £1,150 fee. In his first full season at Burnley he scored a record 32 League goals and in the following 1912–13 promotion winning season scored 31 and for a third consecutive season became leading League goalscorer with 16.

2. **A.** It was Teddy Hodgson who made the pass to Bert Freeman in the 58th minute to score the winning FA Cup winning goal in the 1914 final against Liverpool. In modern day terms, this would have been classed as an assist.

3. **A.** Herbert Bamlett was in indeed the youngest to have refereed an FA Cup Final in 1914. He was in fact the official who abandoned the 4th round FA Cup tie at Turf Moor against eventual 1909 winners Manchester United when after 72 minutes of play, with Burnley 1–0, up called off the tie due to treacherous weather conditions.

4. **C.** Burnley completed the season in 12th position with 12 games won 12 games drawn and 14 games lost in their first season back in the top division since 1900.

5. **B.** The full-back line-up of Bamford and Taylor played together 30 times in the 1913–14 League season and were ever present in 8 the FA Cup ties that were played. The two played together the following season another 34 times before the outbreak of World War 1.

6. **C.** Bert Freeman was top League goalscorer with 16 that season. In his early days, he played for London league side Woolwich Arsenal before moving to Everton where in the 1908–09 season broke the all-time League record scoring a total of 38 goals. He also had the honour or being selected for England.

7. **A.** King George V was in fact the first monarch to attend an FA Cup Final. Tommy Boyle the Burnley captain had the honour of accepting the trophy from him and it would be the last time that the Final would be played at the old Crystal Palace ground.

8. **A.** The Burnley FA Cup winning side of 1914 would in fact never ever play together again. They played together in two league games, the first against Everton and the following day against Derby County, In the semi-final replay against Sheffield United and in the Final itself, making it a total of four games.

9. **C.** The League Champions in the 1913–14 season were rivals Blackburn Rovers who won it from second placed Aston Villa by a clear seven points. In the following season, Blackburn Rovers finished in third place on goal average with 43 points with Burnley also on 43 points in 4th place . Three others clubs also finished with 43 points.

10 **C.** Burnley captain Tommy Boyle scored the winning goal in the replayed FA Cup semi-final against Sheffield United at Goodison Park in the 75 minute of play to book their place in the Final against Liverpool on 25 April 1914.

Quiz 18 Answers and Facts

1. **B.** In the 1946–47 season, owing to the atrocious weather conditions throughout the season, the fixture pile up meant that after Burnley having played in that season's F A Cup Final, had to play a further seven league fixtures with the final game at Millwall on 7 June with the result 1–1. Billy Morris scored the equaliser for Burnley in the second half of play, the first player to do so.

2. **A.** Harry Windle was chairman of Burnley for a total of 21 years from June 1909 till March 1930. He saw the transformation of the club from being a second division club to being one the best in English football. Burnley were unfortunately relegated a month after he retired handing over the chairmanship to William E. Bracewell.

3. **B.** Billy Watson was the first Burnley player to have enlisted in the services during World War One. He joined the Royal Army Service Corp. Unlike two Burnley players Teddy Hodgson and William Pickering who both became casualties of war, he came unscathed throughout.

4. **C.** Richard Lindley made a total of 132 appearances for Burnley scoring a total of 37 goals in his four years during World War One. His closest rival was Bert Freeman who made 76 appearances scoring 39 goals.

5 **C.** Steve Davis was Burnley's record £ 800,000 signing in December 1998 when the club signed him for the third time from Luton Town and he made his first reappearance at Turf Moor against Walsall on 2 January 1999, a game which remained goalless .

6 **C.** Steve Davis was Burnley's record outgoing signing when he signed for Luton Town in July 1995 for £750,000. In his three spells at Burnley, he made 381 plus appearances scoring a total of 47 goals before joining Blackpool in July 2003.

7. **A.** Burnley's first opponents in the inaugural season of the of the Football League Cup were Cardiff City at Ninian Park and Burnley beat them 4–0 on 24 October 1960. Burnley that season progressed to the semi-finals where they were beaten by eventual winners Aston Villa.

8 **B.** Billy Elliott was the record £25,000 signing from Bradford Park Avenue in August 1951 and made his league debut at Middlesbrough on 1 September which resulted in a 0–5 defeat. He made a total of 82 senior appearances before joining Sunderland in June 1953 for a £26,000 fee.

9. **A.** Burnley, when winning the League Championship of 1960 topped the division following their final game at Manchester City, they had been in the top four throughout. The last time they had been top of the division was when they beat Manchester United at Turf Moor on 14 March 1953.

10 **A.** James Crabtree had the honour of being the second Burnley player to have been selected for England . He made three appearances against Ireland twice and Scotland whilst at Burnley. In his career, he represented England a total of 14 times.

Quiz 19 Answers and Facts

1. **A.** Ian Wright, who signed for Burnley from Celtic in February 2000, played his first four games without scoring. He played an additional eleven games as substitute and scored four goals .

2. **B.** Burnley would have missed the Second Division runners up slot and not been promoted had Ian Wright not scored the crucial four goals against Brentford, Notts County, Reading and Gillingham, who would have taken their place by a clear four points.

3. **B.** Burnley, following their Championship play-off victory over Sheffield United in the 2008–09 season, played the following Premier League season of 2009–10 in the original team strip of 1960 with the original badge reintroduced which has since been in use for many seasons.

4. **C.** Having been promoted back to the Championship in the 2013–14 season, Burnley went from 23August 2014 to 4 October 2014 without scoring until they went to Leicester City, when in the 39th minute, Michael Kightley scored for Burnley. It was the first for a total of 655 minutes. It included 5 League fixtures and a 0–1 defeat to Sheffield Wednesday in the Football League cup.

5 **C.** In the Championship winning season of 1959–60, 18 players were used with four players making their League debuts. They were left-back Alex Elder who made 34 appearances that season, the others were goalkeeper Jim Furnell who played once, William Marshall who also made one League appearance and Trevor Meredith who made seven appearances which included his valuable contribution when scoring for Burnley in

the final fixture at Manchester City that brought the Championship back to east Lancashire.

6 **A.** The cheapest admission charge for the 1962 FA Cup Final at Wembley on 5 May 1962, which was a standing at either end behind the goal 5/- (25 pence). In the 60 years since, wages have risen 25 times but admission to the final has risen over 200 times.

7 **B.**   Kevin Long remains the longest serving Burnley player as of May 2022 He signed for the club in January 2010 and has made a total of 185 senior appearances as centre-back. He had been loaned out to many other clubs in his twelve years at Burnley which included Accrington Stanley, Rochdale, Portsmouth , Barnsley and MK Dons. He has represented The Republic of Ireland 17 times.

8. **A.**   Burnley paid Barnsley a record £1,150 fee in September 1911 and his debut was against his old club at Oakwell which ended as a 1–1 draw. He became the only Burnley player as captain to have lifted both the FA Cup and League Championship trophy . He went on to be selected for England against Ireland in Belfast on 15 February 1913. He made over 236 senior appearances at centre-half scoring 43 goals before being transferred to Wrexham In April 1923.

9. **C.**   In the 1912–13 season, Burnley went from 2 November 1912 to 25 February 1913 winning 10 consecutive League games. If you also added three FA Cup ties against Leeds City, Gainsborough Trinity and Middlesbrough, the total within those dates would have been 13 consecutive wins.

10. **A.** There was one change to the side that won the 1914 FA Cup when Burnley hosted Bradford City two days later. Outside-left Eddie Mosscrop was unable to play and was replaced by Billy

Watson moving from his left-half position. Levy Thorpe who had joined the club that season took over Billy Watsons left-half position. It remains a fact that the Cup winning side never ever played together again.

Quiz 20 Answers and Facts

1. **A.** Bert Freeman became the first Burnley player to score 100 League goals when on 21 February 1920 he achieved this feat at Derby County scoring in the 30th minute of play. He scored another three goals in the 1919–20 season but made just three League appearances in the League championship season of 1920–21 before moving to Wigan Borough the following year.

2. **C.** Burnley have been involved in a total of 16 penalty shootouts since they were introduced in the 1990's with the first at Turf Moor against Walsall. In the replayed 2nd round FA Cup tie which ended 1–1 after extra time. Burnley won the penalty shootout 4–2. The most common and successful penalty shootout was at Chelsea in November 2008 in the 4th round of the League Cup when both sides finished 1–1 after extra time. The penalty shootout went 5–4 in Burnley's favour thanks to a brilliant save from goalkeeper Brian Jensen. The last one was at Turf Moor on 9 January 1921 against MK Dons in the 3rd round of the FA Cup when both sides finished 1–1 after extra time. Burnley won the shootout 4–3.

3. **B.** Bert Freeman was born in Handsworth and joined Aston Villa for one season in 1905 and was unable to get into the first team squad. He joined London League club Woolwich Arsenal in the same year and in his three seasons their made 44 senior appearances scoring 21 goals. With the London club severely in debt, had to sell to survive and Bert Freeman's transfer to Everton was their only option. In his three seasons at Everton before joining Burnley he made 86 senior appearances scoring 63 goals.

4. **B.** Burnley have played Manchester United 8 times in the Football League Cup. Their first encounter was on 15 October 1969, which resulted in a 0–0 draw and the club lost the replay at United 0–1.

5. **C.** Charlie Austin became the first Burnley player to score 20 goals in 17 senior appearances in the 2012–13 season when he achieved this feat against Leeds United at Turf Moor on 6 November 2012. The previous record was set by Bert Freeman in the 1911–12 season when he scored 20 goals in 19 senior appearances.

6. **A.** Alex Elder was the youngest Burnley player to have played in all the European competitions when he made his debut at the age of nineteen years and 205 days. He played in a total of four European Cups and four Inter Cities Fairs Cup ties. His final game was at Turf Moor against Eintracht Frankfurt on 18 April 1967 when Burnley went out of the competition beaten 2–3 on aggregate.

7. **A.** Andre Gray was the last player to have scored a hat-trick for Burnley in a League match. It was against Bristol City at Turf Moor on 28 December 2015 with the result being a 4–0 victory for Burnley. He went on to become the seasons top League goalscorer with 25 goals and was part of Burnley's successful 2015–16 championship winning side.

8. **C.** William Jackson was the first Burnley player to have scored four goals in an away tie when he achieved this feat at Keswick in the Qualifying third round FA Cup tie which resulted in Burnley recording their biggest away win in any senior game. It was on 31 October 1903 when Burnley won the tie 8–0. William Jackson came from Barrow in August 1903 and in his short time at Burnley played a total of 24 senior games scoring

a total of 10 goals. Joe Anderson in the 1920 also repeated that feat at Leicester City on 8 January 1921.

9. **A.** Only one player in the history of Burnley Football Club has had a surname beginning with Z. The footballer in question was Robert Zelem who signed for Burnley from Wolverhampton Wanderers in August 1987 as a centre-half. He played a total of 23 plus senior games before being released in May 1989.

10 **C.** The first Burnley player to have scored at Wembley was Jimmy Robson who scored for Burnley in the 49th minute against FA Cup Holders Tottenham Hotspur in the final of 1962. It was the 100th goal to have been scored in a Wembley Final but Burnley were finally beaten 1–3 and became double runners up in both Cup and League competitions.

Quiz 21 Answers and Facts

1. **A.** Burnley's Matej Vydra represented his country The Czech Republic, a total of 13 times in the 2020–21 season, this is more than any other Burnley player has achieved. He played against Cyprus, Israel twice, Scotland twice, Germany, Slovakia, Estonia, Belgium, Wales, Italy, England and Denmark. He was substitute in ten of these Internationals and three of these were in the 2020 European Nations Finals that were played in 1921.

2. **B** There have been a total of 10 Burnley players with the surname Taylor. Joe Taylor, a half-back the first, and up to the end of the 1906-07 season he had made a total of 352 senior appearances for Burnley . David Taylor who played for Burnley in the 1914 FA Cup Final was a hard and solid full-back and made a total of 250 senior appearances. From 1920 to 1939, there were Archie Taylor, Fred Taylor and Alan Taylor. Alan Taylor, Ex-West Ham United forward, came to Burnley in 1984 and made 71 plus appearances for Burnley scoring 32 goals. Steve Taylor joined Burnley in 1980 and made 164 plus appearances scoring 52 goals and was followed by Gareth Taylor the Welsh international who joined Burnley in 2001 and made a total of 98 plus appearances scoring 37 goals. In 2016, another ex-West Ham United player Matt Taylor joined Burnley and was followed by Charlie Taylor who joined the Club from Leeds United.

3. **B.** Alex Stewart was the first Burnley player to have been sent. off in a League game . It was on 12 December 1891 at Turf Moor against rivals Blackburn Rovers. Burnley were leading 3-0 and tempers were rising when Blackburn's Joe Lofthouse badly fouled full back Sandy Lang. All hell broke out with Alex Stewart knocking Lofthouse to the ground. Both sets of players were sent off but things got even worse with Rovers, who were

reduced to seven men, decided to walk off due to the atrocious weather conditions with the match postponed and the result staying as it was, 3–0 to Burnley.

4. **C.**   Burnley introduced the new strip of White shirts and black Shorts at the beginning of the 1935–36 season and wore the strip for a total of eleven years. Because league fixtures were stopped from 1939 till 1946, the strip was used in only four seasons of League Football. but still used in the two FA Cup ties against Stoke City in January 1946.

5. **C.**   Jack Hillman had the unwanted honour of being the first Burnley player to have conceded a penalty in a league game. It was at Sunderland on 21 November 1991 when they were awarded a penalty under the new rules introduced that season. Sunderland were awarded a penalty after Burnley's James Mathew fouled the Sunderland centre-forward. Sunderland's Hugh Wilson slotted the ball past Jack Hillman but later in the game Hillman saved a second penalty from the same penalty taker. Jack Hillman was also the first England goalkeeper to have conceded a penalty on the same ground against Ireland eight years later.

6 **C.**   Paul Fletcher was the leading League goalscorer in the 1972–73 season with 15 goals scored in the Second Division championship winning season. He repeated this the following season Division One season . In his nine years at the club, he made 349 plus appearances scoring a total of 86 goals.

7. **B.**   In the 1971–72 season, Burnley hosted Watford on 8 April 1972 who were bottom of the Second Division. It was the worst post war attendance with just 8,695 witnessing Burnley beating Watford 3–0. In the following four fixtures left to play, Burnley won all of them which went on to be a six game winning run .

8. **C.**   Billy Hamilton became the first Burnley player to score for his country in the World Cup Finals in 1982 on 11 July 1982 against

Austria when he scored both goals for Northern Ireland in their 2–2 drawn game. He made a total of 34 international appearances for Northern Ireland whilst at Burnley and scored a total of five goals.

9. **A.** Burnley who were formed as an Association Football Club in May 1882 celebrated Their 125-year anniversary in 2007. They had played a total of 4,392 League games Won 1,696. Drawn 1,063. Lost 1,633. Scored 6,499. Conceded 4,884.at the end of the 2006–07 season.

10. **C.** Brian Jensen having played for Burnley for 10 years, made a total of 306 senior appearances before signing for Bury. He then went on to play for Crawley Town and Mansfield Town. He will be remembered for the penalty shootout save against Chelsea in November 2008 in the 4th round of the Football League Cup.

Quiz 22 Answers and Facts

1 **A.** Pat Gallocher was the first to score in Burnley's very first League game at Preston North End on 8 September 1888. He scored for Burnley in the 21st minute when Preston were leading 2–0. The second Burnley goal was scored by Fred Poland in the 89th minute with the final result 5–2 to Preston North End.

2. **A.** Fred Poland was to score Burnley's first ever League goal at Turf Moor in the clubs fifth League game of the season against Bolton Wanderers on 6 October 1888 when scoring in the 5th minute and also added another in the 33rd minute with Burnley winning their second game of the season 4–1. Having made eight League appearances, Fred Poland was requested to play in goal in the clubs first home League fixture against Blackburn Rovers at Turf Moor on 3rd December 1988 and conceded seven goals in a 1–7 defeat for Burnley. For some reason unbeknown, he never ever made another appearance for Burnley.

3. **B.** The second Burnley player to have scored a hat-trick in a League game was Claude Lambie against Bolton Wanderers on 1 March 1890 at Turf Moor when scoring in the 2nd the 22nd and the 47th minute in the clubs 7–0 victory. It was only his third League game for Burnley having been purchased from Glasgow Thistle in the January of 1890. He left Burnley the following March 1891 to join Scottish Club Clyde having made 31 senior appearances scoring a total of 22 goals.

4 **C.** Claude Lambie was the first Burnley player to have scored four goals in a League game when on 15 November 1890 against Derby County at Turf Moor in the clubs 6–1 victory. Claude

Lambie the week previous also scored a hat-trick at Aston Villa in a game which ended 4–4 and he became the seasons top league goalscorer with 16 goals in the number nine position.

5. **A.** Jimmy Ross became the first Burnley player to score five goals in a league game against Loughborough at Turf Moor on 28 March 1898 when beating them 9–3 which became the clubs largest ever aggregate. Burnley went on to win the Second Division that season winning promotion via the Test Match system in place at the time. Jimmy Ross one of the Preston North End 'Invincibles' became the clubs highest goal scorer in a season when netting 23 times

6. **A.** Andy Lochhead became the first Burnley player to have scored five goals twice for Burnley in a senior game, firstly against Chelsea at Turf Moor on 24 April 1965 in the Clubs 6–2 beating of the London side. The following 1965–66 season, he repeated this feat in the clubs 7–0 beating of Bournemouth and Boscombe Athletic in the replayed third round FA Cup tie at Turf Moor on 25 January 1966.

7 **C.** Sandy Lang became the first Burnley player to make 100 league appearances for Burnley on 26 November 1892 at Turf Moor against Nottingham Forest which ended 1–1. In his seven seasons at Burnley, local born full-back Sandy Lang played a total of 134 senior appearances before being released in April 1895.

8. **B.** Louis Page became the first Burnley player to have scored six goals in a League game when relegation threatened Burnley met Birmingham on their home soil on 10 April 1926. Louis Page had been moved from his outside-left to the centre-forward position vacated by Tom Roberts. Three first half goals were scored followed by another second half three goals to

make it a double hat-trick. The final result was 7–1 to Burnley, although it helped them from relegation they met a different away side nine days later when losing 1–6 to Sheffield United.

9. **C.** Burnley club captain Tommy Boyle was the first player to have scored for the club following the resumption of league football following World War One. It was in the second league fixture at Bolton Wanderers on 1 September 1919 when scoring a penalty in the 49th minute.

10. **B.** Frank Kippax became the first Burnley player to score for the club following World War Two. It was in the opening game at Turf Moor against Coventry City on 31 August 1946 which resulted in a 1–1 draw. Outside-left player Frank Kippax made a total of 35 senior appearances that season including the FA Cup Final against Charlton Athletic.

Quiz 23 Answers and Facts

1. **B.** Paul Barnes was exchanged for Andy Payton in January 1998 having made 73 plus senior appearances scoring 31 goals in his season and a half stay. In Andy Payton's 19 League appearances for that season he scored a total of nine goals.

2. **A.** Burnley have played a total of 12 FA Cup semi-finals including replays. The first semi- final which was replayed was against Sunderland in 1913 where they lost 2–3 at St Andrews.

   The third semi-final which was also replayed was at Goodison Park where Burnley won 1–0 against Sheffield United to reach the final.

   The fifth semi-final was against Aston Villa where they lost 0–3 at Bramall Lane in 1924.

   The sixth semi-final was in 1935 when they were beaten by Sheffield Wednesday at Villa Park.0–3.

   The seventh which had to be replayed was against Liverpool and victory was made in the when they beat them 1–0 at Main Road Manchester to go to the final.

   The ninth semi-final was against Tottenham Hotspur in 1961 where Burnley were beaten 0–3 at Villa Park.

   It took a replay against Fulham in 1962 at Filbert Street to make it eleven semi-finals played with the twelfth against Newcastle United in 1974 where Burnley were beaten 0-2 at Hillsborough.

3 **C.** Chris Wood scored a total of 10 league goals in the 2017–18 season. His first goal for Burnley that season was at Wembley against Tottenham Hotspur where he equalised in the 90th

minute of play and repeated it in the following home game against Crystal Palace on 10 September 2017. He was the seasons top League goalscorer with 10 goals and scored another from a penalty against Leeds United at Turf Moor in the third round of the EFL cup .

4. **C.** Tommy Lawton who was the youngest ever Burnley player to have played league football for Burnley at the age of 16 years 163 days when he made his debut as centre-forward against Doncaster Rovers at Turf Moor on 28 March 1936, still only an amateur. The £7,000 bid from Everton in January 1937 was too tempting to turn down and the deal was completed at the beginning of that month.

5 **C.** Burnley reserves first won the Central League in the 1948–49 season, winning the division with 60 points. They did it in 1892–93 and 1893–94 To win the North East Lancashire League. They were Central League Champions again in the 1961–62 and 1962–63 seasons. The league was reconstructed in the 1999–2000 season as the Premier Division and were relegated from this league in 2003–04 season.

6. **A.** Harry Potts who played a total of 181 senior appearances scoring 50 goals. He scored his one and only hat-trick against the side he would be transferred to on 3 December 1949 at Turf Moor against Everton in the clubs 5–1 win. He had in his career at Burnley been leading league goalscorer three times . He moved to Everton in October 1950 for a club record £ 20,000 fee. The rest is history for the man that would later lead them to the First Division title and bring European glory to Turf Moor.

7. **B.** In 1952, full-back Harry Woodruff would be the clubs second oldest player after Jerry Dawson. He made his final appearances for Burnley at Chelsea on 19 April 1952 at the age

of 39 years and seven days. He made his League debut as centre-half on 14 September 1936 Against Plymouth Argyle at Turf Moor following his transfer from Bradford City in June 1936. He made a total of 292 senior appearances before moving to Workington in July 1952.

8. **B**   There have been only two sets of brothers who have played together In League football but there have been three if you consider the Gair brothers Jack and William who played for Burnley before the Football League was formed. The first two sets of brothers to play together in league football were David and Jack Walders who first played in the home League game against West Bromwich Albion on 3 September 1904. The second set were Vincent and Richard Overson who first played together in the home league fixture against Orient on 3 November 1979 with Richard coming on as substitute .

9 **C.**   Bob Lord was the longest serving Chairman of Burnley Football Club. Lord a Local butcher who owned a string of shops in the Burnley area was appointed club chairman in June 1955. He was not always a popular figure and said what he thought with his prediction regarding City sides eventually taking over the league was a fact. Due to ill health, he stepped down from his post in October 1981 after Serving the club for over a quarter of a century and was the longest ever Burnley Chairman.

10. **A.**   The first team that Burnley beat in the FA Cup competition were Darwen Old Wanderers at Turf Moor on 15 October 1887 beating them 4–0 . The previous season, they drew twice against Astley Bridge with both clubs deciding to withdraw from the competition. It was comfort to know that they got revenge over the team that beat them two years previously 0–11.

Quiz 24 Answers and Facts

1. **A.** Steve Davis was Burnley's record £800,000 purchase from Luton Town in December 1998 and it was the third time that he re-joined the club. His correct Christian name was Stephen as previously there was a Steven Davis when they played together in the late nineteen eighties He was also the record outgoing transfer player when he went to Luton Town previously. He made a total of 381 plus appearances as a forward scoring 47 goals.

2. **A.** Burnley's 4,000th League game was at Turf Moor on 19 December against Northampton Town in a Division Two fixture. The result was a 0–2 defeat that put Burnley amongst the relegation candidates into nineteenth position. It was also the 2,000th league game to be played at Turf Moor.

3. **C.** Willie Morgan who was signed for Burnley as a junior in 1961 was transferred to Manchester United in August 1968 for a £117,000. He made a total of 215 senior appearances up till that transfer but when he returned to Burnley for a second time in June 1975, he made a further 16 plus appearances before joining Bolton Wanderers in the March of 1976.

4. **B.** At the footballer of the year ceremony for the 1961–62 season, Burnley and Northern Ireland forward Jimmy McIlroy was voted runner up to team-mate and Captain Jimmy Adamson in a season that McIlroy was runner up in three events that season losing out in the League and beaten Wembley FA Cup finalists .

5 **A.** When Jimmy Robson scored five goals against Nottingham Forest at Turf Moor on 21 November 1959, the final score was 8–0 to Burnley with the other three scored by Ray Pointer who scored twice and Brian Pilkington who scored once. It was the

third highest score for Burnley in a home League fixture and equals the 8–2 win over Forest in November 1922.

6 **A.** Loyal servant trainer and footballer Charlie Bates first came to Burnley in May 1910 as a player and made a total of 15 League appearances scoring five times before becoming assistant trainer up until the beginning of World War One . When football recommenced in the 1919–20 season. he took over as trainer and experienced the highs and lows of the Twenties and Thirties. At the end of the 1933–34 season, it was decided to dispense of his services having been the clubs most loyal servant after a period of 24 years.

7. **B.** Record breaking penalty taker Andy McCluggage scored a total of 24 penalties in all senior games . He joined Burnley in May 1925 from Bradford Park Avenue as a half-back and made a total of 213 senior appearances before moving back to Northern Ireland in September 1931. All his 24 goals came from Penalties.

8. **C.** Of the 24 penalties that Northern Ireland international scored for Burnley, 22 were scored in the League and the remaining two from the FA Cup ties that were played. He was selected for Northern Ireland 11 times whilst at Burnley. He has held these records with only Peter Noble and Graham Alexander very close.

9. **A.** Burnley began the 1972–73 second division season having not been beaten in the first 16 League fixtures. Of these seven were won and nine were drawn that put Burnley at the top of the division. The run ended on 11 November 1972 against Orient at Turf Moor when they were defeated 1–2.

10 **B.** Leighton James who came to Burnley in February 1970 as an apprentice had a total of three spells at the club. In his 331 plus League appearances for Burnley scored a total of 66 goals. He was released by Burnley in May 1989 having also

represented Wales whilst at the club 23 times scoring three goals.

Quiz 25 Answers and Facts

1. **C.** Jay Rodriguez scored four goals against Burton Albion in the first round of the Football League Cup at Turf Moor on 9 August 2011 with two of these from penalties. The tie went to extra time at 3–3 with Jay Rodriguez adding two and with one goal from Ross Wallace to make it 6–3 to Burnley. Jay Rodriguez scored a total of 21 goals in all his senior appearances that 2011–12 season.

2. **A.** Peter Noble was the last player to score four goals and not be on the winning side. It was in the Division One fixture at Turf Moor on 13th September 1975 against Norwich City which ended 4–4. As a half-back, It was remarkable that he was such a prolific goalscorer and he added a further three hat-tricks in four seasons at Burnley.

3. **B.** It was full-back John Angus who scored just four goals in his 17 years at Burnley. In one League fixture at Highbury on 17 October 1964, John scored both of Burnley's goals in the 60th and 65th minutes. It was the clubs 2500 league game but Arsenal were too good for them that day winning the game 3–2

4 **C.** Billy Holden scored 4 goals for Burnley at Turf Moor against Sunderland on 11 April 1953. Billy Morris, had the previous season scored at Turf Moor on 8 September 1951. They became the 9th and 10th players to have scored four or more times for Burnley in a League game.

5. **A.** When at the auction house, the Mechanics institute in Burnley, in September 1922, two lots of land came up for sale. Lot number 55 was two pieces of land, Turf Moor and the Cricket Field were auctioned. The winning bidder was Burnley Football Cub who successfully purchased them both for a sum of £4,500.

6. **C.** George Beel arguably Burnley's greatest ever goalscorer scored a total of nine FA Cup goals for the club in his nine years of service. The 179 league goalscorer first opened up his FA Cup scoring account against Swindon Town in the fourth round tie at Turf Moor on 12 March 1924 scoring twice. He scored a further two goals against Cardiff City in the third round on 9 January 1926. He scored his fifth goal against Grimsby Town before scoring a further two goals in the fourth round tie at Fulham on 29 January 1927. His eighth and ninth FA Cup goals came in the 1928–29 season against Sheffield United and Swindon Town.

7 **C.** Popular Burnley author Dave Thomas has written many publications on the subject which are both entertaining and easy reading. His first was *It's Burnley Not Barcelona* which became a good seller. One of his best is the life and times of ex Burnley Chairman Bob Lord titled *Bob Lord of Burnley.* and there will be many more from the Burnley author from Yorkshire.

8. **C.** The Anglo- Scottish Cup, which replaced the Texaco cup, Burnley first played in the competition in the 1976–77 season with the first game against Blackburn Rovers at Ewood Park on 7 August 1976. In the third 1978–79 season of Burnley's involvement in this competition, they went as far as the Final having beaten Preston North End, Blackpool, Blackburn Rovers, Celtic twice, Mansfield Town twice and Oldham Athletic twice in the two legged final. Burnley won this competition 4–2 on aggregate.

9. **A.** Tommy Lawton, was Burnley's youngest player, was selected for England a total of 23 times following his transfer to Everton. He was selected for England in 1938 and was selected for a total of ten seasons

10. **B.** Tommy Lawton scored a total of 22 goals for England in his 10 years of team selection. He was a prolific header of the ball and

scored on a regular basis for the many clubs he played for after leaving Everton, which Including Chelsea, Notts County, Brentford and Arsenal.

Quiz 26 Answers and Facts

1. **A.** There have been just three Burnley players who have been clubs leading league goalscorers four times or more . The first was Bert Freeman in the 1911–12 season with 32 and he repeated this the following two seasons with 31 and 16 goals. In the 1919–20 season, he scored 12. The second player to do this was George Beel who was first leading league goalscorer in 1923–24 with 19 and continued for a further five seasons to the 1931–32 season having been top league goalscorer six times The third and final player was Billy Hamilton who was first leading League goalscorer in the 1979–80 season with seven. He was top league goalscorer a further three times, the last was in the 1983–84 season with 18.

2. **C.** Herbie Arthur the Blackburn Rovers and England goalkeeper was the one and only Rovers player left on the field of play on 12 December 1891 at Turf Moor. The weather conditions were atrocious with some of the Blackburn Rovers players refusing to participate in the second half but the referee blew to commence the game with goalkeeper Herbie Arthur in this I'll tempered match at one time the only Rovers player left . The referee had had enough and abandoned the game with the 3–0 result to Burnley left intact.

3. **B.** George Brown Burnley's centre forward in the 1934–35 season scored a total of 14 goals from 16 league games. He made his league debut for Burnley against Manchester United at Turf Moor on 6 October 1934 having been purchased from Aston Villa. He completed this feat in his 16th game against Notts County at Turf Moor on 5 January 1935 in a 4–0 home win. He was the seasons leading club league goalscorer with 21.

4. **A.** Burnley achieved a total of 91 league goals scored in the 1926–27 season bettering the 88 league goals scored in the 1912–13

season. George Beel was the leading league goalscorer with 24 followed by Louis Page with 13. It was a very good season for Burnley who finished the season in 5th position in the first division table having avoided relegation the season previous.

5. A.   David Taylor who made a total of 250 senior appearances for Burnley from 1911 to 1924 took over the managers roll at St Johnstone in May 1924. He was a member of the club's 1914 FA Cup winning side and appeared 11 times for Burnley in the League Championship winning side of 1921.

6. **C.**   7 Burnley players played in both the 1914 FA Cup Final and the League Championship side of 1921. They were full-back David Taylor (11), half-backs. George Halley (26) Tommy Boyle (38) Billy Watson (42), forwards Bert Freeman (3). Eddie Mosscrop (14) and Willie Nesbitt (40).

7. **B.**   The record 30 undefeated league games that Burnley achieved in the 1920–21 season was broken on 26 March 1921 at Manchester City when Burnley were defeated 0–3. With six games to go in this record-breaking Championship season, the club were beaten twice by West Bromwich Albion and Sunderland. The 30 game unbeaten run was ended by Arsenal in the early 2000s

8. **B.**   The one and only FA Cup semi-final to be played at Turf Moor was on 25 March 1922 with Huddersfield Town and Notts County competing for a place in the Final. Huddersfield Town won the tie 2–0 and went on to win the final beating Preston North End 1–0.

9 **B.**   There have been a total of 163 hat-tricks scored by a Burnley player in a senior game since 1888. These include a goalscorer who scores four or five in a game and in Louis Pages six goals scored at Birmingham in 1926 counts as a double hat-trick. The last player to have achieved this was Jay Rodriguez against Rochdale in the EFL cup in the 1921-22 season where he scored four times.

10. **A.** John Bond who joined the Club at the start of the 1983–84 season left at the end of that campaign to join Swansea City. His promises to make Burnley a bigger club came to nothing with the club finishing in their worst position of 12th in division three. He however proved himself at other clubs which included Manchester City, Norwich City and the transformation at Bournemouth and Boscombe Athletic where he changed the name to AFC Bournemouth and the club strip from red and white to black and Red stripes.

Quiz 27 Answers and Facts

1. **C.** Sam Vokes became the most capped Burnley player in the 2015–16 season when he made 11 international appearances for Wales. He made appearances against. Cyprus, Israel and Bosnia Herzegovina as substitute, followed by a full internationals against Andorra. and Northern Ireland. He was a sub against Ukraine and Sweden before the European Championships in France 2016, where made full international appearances against Russia and Northern Ireland before being a sub against Belgium where he scored and finally he was a sub against Portugal.

2. **A.** Burnley full-back Michael Duff made a total of 21 international appearances for Northern Ireland whilst at the club. His first appearance was as a sub against Switzerland in Zurich on 18 August 2004. He followed this up the following September against England In Belfast once again as a sub. From then on, he made regular international appearances with his final selection being against Holland in Amsterdam in June 2012.

3. **B.** A total of 10 Burnley players were selected for their country in the 2016–17 season. They were Scott Arfield for Canada, Jeff Hendrick, Robbie Brady, Stephen Ward and Kevin Long for the Republic of Ireland, Michael Keane and Tom Heaton for England, Sam Vokes for Wales, Steven Defour for Belgium and Johann Gudmundsson for Iceland.

4. **C.** Burnley goalkeeping legend Jimmy Strong retired from football in May 1954 having made a total of 285 senior appearances. He was the only Burnley player to date who had made a total of 203 consecutive league appearances, he also holds many other records. When he finally retired he became a poultry farmer near his home in Burnley.

5 **B.** Tommy Boyle is the only Burnley player to have lifted both the FA Cup and League championship trophy, he was born in Barnsley on 29 January 1888. He made a total of 236 senior appearances for Burnley in his twelve years with the club before joining Wrexham in April 1923.

6. **C.** Robbie Blake was sold by Burnley in January 2005 to Birmingham City for a record outgoing sum of £1.25 million. He returned to Burnley from Leeds United in July 2007 for a £250,000 fee. In total, Robbie Blake, in his two spells at Burnley, made 197 League appearances plus 45 as substitute scoring 61 goals.

7. **C.** Burnley's second most capped player is Sam Vokes who was selected for Wales whilst at the club 40 times which was second only to Jimmy McIlroys 51 caps. His first international for Burnley was against Bosnia and Herzegovina on 15 August 2012. His final and 40th international appearance was against Albania on 20 November 2018.

8. **A.** Three Burnley goalkeepers were used in the 2020–21 season. They were Nick Pope who had 33 senior appearances, Bailey Peacock Farrell with eight senior appearances and Will Norris with three senior appearances.

9. **B.** In the five FA Cup ties that Burnley played in the 1956–57 season, Ian Lawson scored in three of these with four against Chesterfield in the third round and a further three against New Brighton in the fourth round. In the fifth round against Huddersfield Town, he scored once more to make it eight goals from four FA Cup ties.

10. **B.** The only occasion that a Brazilian player has played for Burnley was at Huddersfield Town on the opening game of the Championship season 29 July 2022 when new signing from Cercle Brugge, Vitinho made his Burnley debut as a midfielder.

Quiz 28 Answers and Facts

1. **A.** In the 1982–83 season, Poco Homes become Burnley's first ever shirt sponsor. The agreement throughout football at the time was that these shirts could not be worn in televised games. It was ironic as Burnley made it to the latter stages of both major cup competitions. The deal lasted for one season only, with the relegated side opting for the TSB Bank for the following division three campaign

2. **C.** Harry Potts, who was transferred to Everton October 1950, was replaced by a young Jimmy McIlroy who made his League debut at Sunderland on 21 October 1950. Harry Potts who signed for Burnley as a junior in November 1937 made a total of 181 senior appearances for Burnley scoring 50 goals.

3. **B.** In the Division one league game against Preston North End on Christmas Day 1953, at Turf Moor, both Burnley and North Ends goalkeepers were brothers, with Des in goal for Burnley and George for Preston. The result was a 2–1 win for Burnley that was reversed the following day at Deepdale. Brother George had the honour that season of becoming the Preston North End keeper in that seasons FA Cup Final where the lost to West Bromwich Albion 2–3.

4. **C.** As of 18 November 2020, both Burnley goalkeepers Danny Coyne and Bailey Peacock-Farrell had made 10 international appearances for Burnley with both keepers sharing the club record. Danny Coyne had made 10 appearances for Wales up to end of May 2007. The record was equalled on 18 November 2020 when Peacock Farrell played for Northern Ireland against Romania in Belfast.

5. **C.** The Longside, at the start of the 1954–55 season, was roofed over at a cost of £20,000 in time for the beginning of the first

League fixture at Turf Moor on 21 August 1954 against Cardiff City which resulted in a 1–0 win for Burnley .

6. **C.** Ralph Coates was the last Burnley player to have represented the Football League in the 1970–71 season against the Scottish League and the Irish League. He had in total represented the Football League whilst at Burnley four times, as well representing England twice in full Internationals.

7. **A.** When Jimmy McIlroy won his eleventh international cap for Northern Ireland, against Scotland on 3rd November 1954, he shared the record with England's Bob Kelly and Northern Ireland's Andy McCluggage. Jimmy McIlroy would eventually surpass this record setting his own at 51 caps whilst a Burnley player.

8 **A.** Arthur Bell and Peter Kippax were the only two Burnley amateurs to have represented England amateurs. Arthur Bell who played for Burnley making 104 senior appearances from 1902 to 1909 was a very respected member of society and was a local architect, which involved him in future building plans at Turf Moor. Peter Kippax the second amateur international for England joining Burnley in 1940 as a junior. Having made 43 senior appearances which included an appearance for Burnley in the 1947 FA Cup Final, he went on to join Liverpool in 1949.

9 **B.** Eight of the Burnley youth team that beat Coventry City in 1968 went on to make first team selection for Burnley. Club captain Michael Docherty made a total of 168 plus senior appearances with Steve Kindon making 212 plus senior appearances scoring 58 goals. Dave Thomas made 175 plus senior appearances scoring 23 times, with Eric Probert making 67 plus appearances scoring 11. Alan West made 47 plus senior appearances with Eddie Cliff making 24 senior appearances. Wilf Wrigley and Peter Jones had a handful of senior appearances which meant a total of eight members of the winning side became first team players.

10. **C.** Burnley and Blackburn Rovers have played a total of 88 times against each other up to 30 May 2022. The first game was at Turf Moor on 3 November 1888 when Blackburn Rovers ran riot beating Burnley 1–7. The result for Burnley the following League season was no better when they were beaten 1–6. On 18 April 1896, Burnley got the upper hand beating their rivals 6–0 at Turf Moor. The biggest aggregate was at Ewood Park on 9 November 1929 when Blackburn Rovers beat Burnley 8–3. To date Burnley have won 35. Drawn 16 and Lost 37 in league games.

Quiz 29 Answers and Facts

1. **A.** Burnley have won a total of 1,919 league games since their first win at Bolton Wanderers on 15 September 1888 which resulted 4–3. The last win for Burnley was at Watford on 30 April 2022 which resulted in a 2–1 victory.

2. **B.** Burnley have drawn a total of 1,234 league games with the first against Everton at Turf Moor on 17 November 1888. The last one to be drawn was at the London Stadium against West Ham United which ended 1–1.

3. **A.** Burnley have lost a total of 1,865 league games since the first, which was their very first game at Preston North End on 8 September 1888 which resulted in a 2–5 defeat. The final defeat was at Turf Moor on 22 May 2022 when they were beaten 1–2 by Newcastle United.

4. **C.** Burnley have scored a total of 7,266 league goals since the first, scored by Pat Gallocher at Preston North End on 8 September 1888 in the clubs very first league game. The last player to score for Burnley was Maxwel Cornet against Newcastle United at Turf Moor on 22 May 2022.

5 **B.** Burnley since their first league game, where they conceded five goals at Preston North End on 8 September 1888 have conceded a total of 5,717 goals. The first person to concede was Burnley keeper W. Smith. The last goalkeeper to concede was Nick Pope against Newcastle United at Turf Moor on 22 May 2022.

6. **B.** Burnley have been relegated from the First Division/Premier League eight times. The first was in the 1896–97 season when finishing bottom of 16 clubs. The second time was in the 1899–

1900 season when finishing second from bottom with Glossop. The third relegation came in the 1929–30 season when second from bottom with Everton. The fourth was in the 1970–71 season when once again second from bottom with Blackpool. The fifth relegation was in the 1975–76 season when second from bottom with Sheffield United. In the 2009–10 season , they were relegated along with Hull City and Portsmouth. The club's seventh came in the 2014–15 season when relegated with Hull City and Queens Park Rangers. The eighth relegation from the top flight came at the end of the 2021–22 season when relegated with Watford and Norwich City.

7. **A.**   Burnley have been bottom of the First division in the 1897 season and were bottom of the Second Division in 1903. In the 1896–97 season, they finished bottom with 19 points and were relegated through the test match system, losing to Notts County and Newton Heath over a two-legged affair. They were bottom of the Second Division in the 1902–03 season, level on points with Stockport County with 20. Both sides had to seek re-election but it was the team above them, Doncaster Rovers on 25 points who lost their League status.

8. **A.**   Burnley did in fact celebrate their 140th anniversary having been founded as an Association Football team in 1882. They have won every league title in all the four divisions except the Third Division South and North which was incorporated into the Third Division and Fourth Division in the early sixties.

9. **A.**   Burnley's record post war league attendance was on 11 October 1947 against Blackpool when 52,869 witnessed a 1–0 win for Burnley. It was about 1,906 short of the record pre-war attendance against Huddersfield Town in February 1924 which was a Third round FA Cup tie. The post war record for a cup tie

at Turf Moor stands at 52,850 against Bradford City in February 1960.

10. **C.** The attendance at the Sherpa Van Final (Football League Trophy) on 29 May 1988 was 80,841. The result was a 2–0 win for Wolverhampton Wanderers against Burnley which still remains a record attendance for two Division Four teams.

Quiz 30 Answers and Facts

1 **B.** When Wimbledon moved to Milton Keynes from Plough Lane in September 2003, Burnley were in fact the first opponents at the National Hockey Stadium on 27 September 2003 in the clubs First Division fixture. The result was 2–2 with Robbie Blake scoring two first half goals. He was in fact the first player to score the opening goal in this revamped hockey stadium.

2. **C.** Michael Kightley was transferred to his old club Southend United in August 2017 and scored in his first return match against Blackburn Rovers . He was originally loaned to Burnley from Stoke City in 2013 before being purchased the following season. He made a total of 76 senior appearances and was loaned to Burton Albion before his transfer back to Southend United.

3. **A.** There were a total of 11 games played at Calder Vale before Burnley moved to Turf Moor in February 1883, Their first opponents were Burnley Rovers who they beat 4–0. In their third home game on the old Rugby ground, they lost 0–8 to Astley Bridge which was followed by a Blackburn Rovers A side who beat them 0–10. The final game was against Haslington who they beat 1–0 on 3 February 1883.

4. **A.** Jack Yates who became Burnley's first England International player against Ireland on 2 March 1889 and scored a hat-trick on his International debut. He was transferred from Accrington for the inaugural league game at Preston North End on 8 September 1888 and played a total of 29 League games for Burnley scoring a total of seven goals before being released in April 1894.

5. **B.** Sean Dyche's first game in charge of Burnley was at Turf Moor on 3 November 2012 against Wolverhampton Wanderers, who were beaten 2–0. Sean Dyche was a defender in his playing days under Brian Clough at Nottingham Forest and eventually Chesterfield and Millwall. His first managerial post was at Watford but was unfortunately dismissed before eventually joining Burnley in October 2012 with his assistant Ian Woan. He became one of the club's most successful managers and in his nine years and six months spell took the club twice to promotion to the Premiership as well as taking them into European football for the first time since 1967.

6 **C.** Jack Cork was first loaned to Burnley from Chelsea in the 2010–11 season and made a total of 51 senior appearances. He moved to Burnley on a permanent basis having been transferred from Swansea City in 2017. He has up to May 2022 made a further total of 141 senior appearances as well as an International appearance for England against Germany as a substitute in November 2017.

7 **C.** Burnley last played a League fixture on Christmas Day in 1957 at Turf Moor against Manchester City which ended 2–1 to Burnley. The return fixture at Main Road on the Boxing Day ended in a 1–4 defeat to Burnley.

8. **B.** Everton were relegated along with Burnley at the end of the 1929–30 season as the bottom club in the First division. It was a turning point in the Merseysider's success having won the Second division the following season and would eventually become FA Cup winners in 1933 and also league champions in 1939.

9 **C.** Jimmy Mullen became Burnley manager in October 1991, having taken over from Frank Casper and was in the managerial role at Burnley until February 1996. He was

responsible for the club's promotion from the Fourth division in 1992 and their play-off final win against Stockport County in 1994 becoming the first Burnley manager to do it twice. He was at Burnley for a total of 5 seasons.

10. **A.** The last League game before the outbreak of World War Two was at Birmingham on 2 September which ended in a 0–2 defeat. The records of the two games that were played were expunged and were played again following the end of the hostilities of war in 1946. The second Division two league fixture at a now renamed Birmingham City ended in a 2–0 victory for Burnley on 7 September 1946. Only two player were involved in both games with Arthur Woodruff and George Bray the surviving two.

Quiz 31 Answers and Facts

1. **A.** It is believed that Burnley first used the nickname the Clarets in the late sixties. In previous years, they have been called the Royalites, the Cotton Weavers, the Turfites, the Moorites and many more along the way.

2. **A.** It was a fact that two Burnley sides played at the same time. In the clubs first ever senior game against Darwen Old Wanderers in the FA Cup tie which ended in the clubs biggest ever defeat losing 0–11 with only a second non-professional team allowed to participate. At Turf Moor at the same time, Wolverhampton Wanderers we're the visitors and Burnley triumphed 4–1 on 17 October 1885.

3. **C.** Goalkeeper Jimmy Strong, who had represented Burnley several times, in the Second World War fixtures was a guest player from Walsall FC and signed for Burnley in January 1946. He became the clubs first player to have made 203 consecutive League appearances and broke numerous records in his 285 senior appearances.

4. **C.** Burnley first participated in the Anglo Scottish Cup competition in the 1976-77 season with the first tie against Blackburn Rovers at Ewood Park on 7 August 1976 which ended 1–1. The final tie in this competition was played at Turf Moor on 5 August 1980 which ended 1–1 against Shrewsbury Town. They played a total of 21 ties over this 4-year period winning the competition against Oldham Athletic 4-2 on aggregate in a two-legged final in 1978.

5. **B.** James McConnell was Burnley's first recorded goalkeeper to have played in a senior competition when he played two FA Cup ties in 1886–87 season against Astley Bridge with both ties

ending 3–3 and 2–2. Both clubs subsequently withdrew from the competition.

6. **A.** James Clayton was Burnley's leading League goalscorer with 10 in the 1938–39 season and because he was such a talented player, the outbreak of the Second World War curtailed his future ambitions. He scored a hat-trick against Tranmere Rovers at Turf Moor on 26 November 1938, the last until Billy Morris scored one at Coventry City on 28 December 1946, eight years later.

7. **C.** Ray Pointer was the second highest League goalscorer with 118 with George Beel the highest with 179. Ray Pointer was a very popular player with the Burnley fans and in his eight seasons at the club scored a total of 132 goals from 270 senior appearances before joining Bury in August 1965.

8. **B.** The highest ever score that Burnley beat Blackburn Rovers by at Turf Moor in a League match was on 18 April 1896 in a First division fixture , beating their local rivals 6–0. The Burnley scorers that afternoon were Tom Nicol with a hat-trick , Hugh Robertson with two and Walter Place senior with one.

9. **A.** The only other two teams to have won all four divisional leagues are Wolverhampton Wanderers and Preston North End. Like Burnley, the other two were founder members of the Football League in the 1888–89 season and Burnley and Preston North End have won the league title twice with Wolverhampton Wanderers winning it three times.

10. **C.** Burnley's record signing in October 1938 was James Clayton from Aston Villa for a £3,500 fee. He played a total of 16 League games in the 1938–39 season scoring 10 goals before the outbreak of the Second World War . Throughout the war, he made a total of 12 senior appearances for Burnley before retiring.

Quiz 32 Answers and Facts

1 **C.**   Steve Kindon was Burnley's leading league goalscorer twice. He first achieved this feat in the 1969–70 season with 17 goals scored and followed this up eight seasons later in the 1977–78 season with 12. From 1972 till 1977, he was at Wolverhampton Wanderers before returning to Burnley for a second time. In 1979, he was transferred to Huddersfield Town .

2. **C.**   Burnley were represented with a total of five players for the World Cup qualifier in Cardiff, with Wales taking on the Republic of Ireland on 9 October 2017. Playing for the Republic were Robbie Brady, Kevin Long, Stephen Ward and Jeff Hendrick. Selected for Wales was Sam Vokes with the result a 1–0 victory for the Republic of Ireland.

3. **C.**   The previous time that Burnley beat Everton at Goodison Park was in the 1975–76 season when Burnley beat them 3–2 on 31 January 1976 with goals from Peter Noble, Bryan Flynn and Derek Scott. The season was to end in relegation and would be the last time they would meet in a league fixture at Goodison Park until 28 December 2009 nearly 33 years later.

4 **A.**   Bolton Wanderers were Burnley's opponents on 13 October 1986 when Prince Albert Victor attended the friendly between the two clubs. and stayed for a total of twenty minutes. The royal party were there to open the newly built hospital in Burnley. The result was a 3–4 defeat for Burnley and for many years later the club were called the Royalites.

5. **C.**   Italian Club AC Milan did in fact bid for the services of Burnley's Jimmy McIlroy in the early sixties. Jimmy McIlroy was given the honour of being the greatest Burnley player of all time. He

played a total of 497 senior games for Burnley scoring 131 goals before signing for Stoke City in 1963.

6. **B.** George Beel was the top goalscorer for Burnley, having played a total of 337 senior appearances scoring 189 goals. His first game, after been transferred from Chesterfield in April 1923 was against Birmingham City on 5 May. His final game was on 6 February 1932 at Turf Moor against Bradford Park Avenue before joining Lincoln City.

7. **C.** George Beel, Burnley's all-time greatest goalscorer scored a total of 11 hat-tricks from a total 316 League games. His first hat-trick was against West Ham United at Turf Moor on 17 November 1923 when beating the London side 5–1. His final hat-trick was at Turf Moor against Wolverhampton Wanderers on 3 February 1931 with the result a 4–2 victory for the Turfites. George Beel was the club's record top scorer with 35 goals in the 1927–28 season which is a record that still stands to this day.

8. **B.** Mike Prosser's *Burnley Goalkeeping Legends* published in August 2019 was the first which had a QR code that could be downloaded and featured every season and every goalscorer from 1888 to 2019.

9. **A.** Besart Berisha the Albanian international was purchased in July 2007 for a total of £340,000 having impressed Burnley in a B international at Turf Moor against England. He was loaned to Rosenborg in Norway a year later having never appeared for Burnley in his time at the club. He did in fact play a total of 10 internationals for Albania whilst at Burnley before joining AC Horsens in January 2009.

10 **B.** Tommy Lawton Burnley youngest ever player scored his only hat trick for the club at Turf Moor on 10 October 1936 against Tottenham Hotspur when beating them 3–1. Within three months, he had signed for Division One Everton for a record £7,000 outgoing fee. He had played a total of 25 League games for Burnley scoring a total of 16 goals.

Quiz 33 Answers and Facts

1. **B.** Alan Brown was the first ex-Burnley player to have managed the club. He took over from Frank Hill in August 1954 and was in his position for a total of three seasons taking them to 10th place in his first season, then into seventh place twice before joining Sunderland as manager. As a player, he made 98 senior appearances before joining Notts County in October 1948 and was captain of the Burnley side that lost to Charlton Athletic in the 1947 FA Cup Final.

2. **B.** Burnley lost a total of 11 league games in the Championship winning season of 1959–60. They suffered two 1–4 home defeats to Blackpool and Manchester United and a 1–6 defeat at Wolverhampton Wanderers, who were their closest rivals for the League Championship that season. The club won the league by just one point, on 55 points with Wolverhampton Wanderers having 54 points.

3. **B.** Former England international player Cliff Britton came to Burnley in May 1945 as the clubs first manager since 1935 and had two seasons in charge before moving on to manage Everton. He had been successful in getting promotion back to the First Division as well as a FA Cup Final in 1947 where they were beaten by the previous seasons beaten finalists, Charlton Athletic. In his second season at Burnley, his team finished third on goal average to second placed Manchester United.

4. **C.** There were 8 Burnley players who made their League debuts against. Huddersfield Town on 29 July 2022. They were Goalkeeper, Arijanet Muric. Defenders, Taylor Harwood Bellis, Ian Maatsen and Vitinho Midfielders, Josh Cullen, Samuel Bastien and Dara Costelloe and Forward, Scott Twine.

5. **C.** Burnley, when they became first members of the Football League in 1888, went a total of 70 League games without a goalless result. On the 71st league match on 7 November 1891 at Wolverhampton Wanderers the result was 0–0 which would be Burnley's only goalless result of the 1891–92 season.

6. **A.** Alan Pace was in fact the 19th Chairman at Burnley when he took over from Mike Garlick in December 2020. Mike Garlick and John Banaszkiewicz were also joint Chairman from 2012 to 2015.

7 **A.** Half back Willie Watson was the only Burnley player made all 42 appearances in the 1920–21 Championship winning season. He was part of the famous half back line-up of Haley, Boyle and Watson. He made a total of 380 senior appearances for Burnley from 1909 to 1925.

8. **B.** The Longside stand was demolished in September 1995 to make way for the new all seater James Hargreaves stand. It had previously had a stand named the Stars stand which Burnley had purchased from the defunct Burnley Union Star Football Club. It had remained open following the removal of that stand and later replaced with another.

9. **B.** Dave Burnley, who was a regular supporter for many years home and away and had not missed a game in 44 years. He changed his name by deed pole to Dave Burnley and named his daughter Claret. He comes from Stoke-on-Trent and due to the corona virus pandemic had to miss his first ever game at Manchester City that was played behind closed doors in 2020.

10 **C.** Both Jimmy McIlroy and John Angus have made a total of 439 League appearances, although one of these from John Angus was as a substitute. John Angus made a total of 520 plus senior appearances with Jimmy McIlroy making a total of 497 senior appearances.

Quiz 34 Answers and Facts

1. **B.** Vincent Kompany was in fact the 29th permanent Burnley manager when he was appointed in June 2022. He was Manchester City's captain, winning many trophies for the club which included FA Cup, Football League Cup and Premiership titles. He made a total of 265 senior appearances for City and was a Belgium international player and had previous managerial experience with Anderlecht in Belgium.

2. **C.** Martin Buchan had the shortest reign as Burnley manager having come to the club with high expectations. He was a Scottish international player and had played over 450 senior games for Manchester United before taking over at Burnley in June 1985. Having experienced just four wins from 13 games, he decided that management was not for him and resigned from his post in October 1985 after just four months in the post.

3. A. Harry Bradshaw was Burnley's first ever manager at the commencement of the 1894–95 season. It had been previously run by a selection committee, the correct title of the post was that of Secretary/Manager. It was long thought that the first manager was Arthur Sutcliffe and was later confirmed that his post was that of Secretary. Harry Bradshaw was in that position for five seasons before moving. to south London second division side Woolwich Arsenal and finally Southern League Fulham.

4. **B.** Fred Dewhurst was the first player to have scored a League goal against Burnley in the opening Football League game at Deepdale when scoring for Preston North End in the second minute of their match on 8 September 1888.

5. **A.** Burnley had their longest winning run in the 1912–13 season which was a total of 10 Division Two matches that went from 16 November 1912 to 25 January 1913 when they were beaten at home by Nottingham Forest 3–5 Burnley finished the season as promoted runners up to Preston North End and were also FA Cup semi-finalists, being beaten by Sunderland

6. **A.** Jimmy McIlroy was the first Burnley player to have scored in European football for club. The first ever tie was against French club Reims at Turf Moor on 16 November 1960 in the European Cup second round first leg, which ended 2–0 to Burnley with goals scored by both Jimmy McIlroy and Jimmy Robson. It was the only goal that McIlroy scored in this competition out of four appearances that season.

7. **C.** Paul Barnes was Burnley's £400,000 record signing in September 1996 from Birmingham City and he made his inside-left debut at Gillingham on 7 September 1996 which ended in a 0–1 defeat. He made 39 plus appearances that season becoming leading league goalscorer with 24. On 5 October 1996 Barnes became the fifth Burnley player to have scored five goals in a game when the club beat Stockport County at Turf Moor 5–2. He made a total of 73 plus senior appearances for Burnley scoring 31 goals before being transferred to Huddersfield Town in January 1998.

8 **C.** On 29 November 1919. Burnley topped the First Division table for the second time in their history having beaten Bradford Park Avenue 1–0 on their own ground. It was the only occasion that they topped the league that season, finishing as runners up to West Bromwich Albion, the eventual Champions. The previous occasion was on 5 September 1898 when they beat Preston North End 3–1 at Turf Moor after their second league game that season.

9. **C.** Nottingham Forest were Burnley's league opponents on 4 November 1922 at Turf Moor when the club recorded the highest ever winning First Division aggregate beating the visitors 8–2 with goals scored from Benny Cross (3). Bob Kelly (2) Billy Watson (2) and Walter Weaver. The highest ever league Division Two aggregate was 9–3 when Burnley beat Loughborough by that score line at Turf Moor on 28 March 1898 with Jimmy Ross becoming the first Burnley player to score five goals in a league game.

10 **B.** Burnley have played a total of 18 European Cup ties since their first on 16 November 1960, when they first competed in the European Cup as League Champions only to be finally beaten in the fourth-round tie against SV Hamburg. The second occasion was when they qualified for the Inter-Cities Fairs Cup in 1966 having finished in third place in the 1965–66 league table and played a total of 8 ties before being finally knocked out by Eintracht Frankfurt 2–3 on aggregate. The third occasion was in the Europa League competition having qualified in seventh place in the 2017–18 Premiership table. Six ties were played, the first at Aberdeen on 26 July 2018 and the final tie was against Olympiacos where they were beaten 2–4 on aggregate.

1. **C.**   The first Burnley manager to have had First Division playing experience was Tom Bromilow, having played over 300 league games for Liverpool as well as being selected for England five times. He joined Burnley as manager in October 1932, having inherited a struggling side and finished in nineteenth place in the Second Division table of 1932–33. The following season the club finished thirteenth and finally twelfth in the 1934–35 season before Bromilow moved on to manage Third Division South Crystal Palace.

2. **A.**   Tommy Willighan was the last Burnley player prior to the outbreak of the Second World War to be selected for his country. He was selected for Northern Ireland against Scotland at Hampden Park on 16 September 1933 where they won Home International match 2–1 He had previously been selected against Wales at Wrexham on 7 December 1932 where they were beaten 1–4.

3. **A.**   Burnley full-back Ben Mee made a total of 351 League appearances after joining the club on loan from Manchester City in July 2011. He made his league debut against Watford on 6 August 2011 and was finally purchased from Manchester City in January 2012 along with Kieran Trippier for an undisclosed fee. He suffered an injury in the 2021–22 season and was assistant to interim manager Mike Jackson following the sacking of Sean Dyche in April 2022.

4. **B.**   Hugh Flack, who made his League debut for Burnley against Bury at Turf Moor on 18 February 1929 was selected for Northern Ireland against Scotland five days later on 23 February 1929 in Belfast where they lost 3–7. It was to be his

only international appearance. Having been purchased from Crusaders in May 1927, the full back played just three games for Burnley before moving to Swansea Town in May 1929.

5. **C.** Burnley manager Tom Bromilow, who resigned his position at the end of the 1934–35 season joined Third Division south side Crystal Palace having taken over the position from former Burnley player Jack Tresadern. He had two spells at Palace before joining Leicester City during World War Two. He finally managed Newport County in 1948.

6 **B.** Jimmy Dunne was the last Burnley player to have scored on his Premier League debut at Leicester City on 20 September 1920. He made a total of three senior appearances for Burnley before joining Queens Park Rangers in July 1921.

7. **B.** There have been five other Burnley players who have scored five or more league goals in one game. Jimmy Ross was the first to do it against Loughborough on 28 March 1898. The second was Joe Anderson against Aston Villa on 5 February 1921. The third was Louis Page who scored five at Birmingham on 10 April 1926 but added a further goal two minutes later in the 62 minute. The fourth was Jimmy Robson against Nottingham Forest on 21 November 1959 with the fifth scored by Andy Lochhead against Chelsea on 24 April 1965.

8 **A.** Burnley went a total of 18 League games without a win in the 2006–07 season. Having beaten Ipswich Town 1–0 on 4 November 2006 they had to wait until the league game against Plymouth Argyle at Turf Moor on 3 April 2007 for their first win, with the result 4–0 to the home side and they continued winning a further four games to the end of that season.

9. **C.** Jay Rodriguez was first leading league goalscorer in the 2010–11 season with 14 goals scored. He was joint overall goalscorer with Chris Eagles both with 15 goals.

10. **B.** Goalkeeper Tom Heaton was the first Burnley player since Martin Dobson in 1974 to have made an appearance for England. He made it as a substitute against Australia at Sunderland on 27 May 2016. Tom Heaton made a further two England appearances, against Spain at Wembley on 15 November 2016 and as a substitute against France in Paris on 13 June 2017.

Quiz 36 Answers and Facts

1. **B.**   Alex Leake, who joined Burnley from Aston Villa in December 1907 had previously made a total of five international appearances for England. He made a total of 90 senior appearances for Burnley at centre-half. before moving to Wednesbury in June 2010.

2 **A.**   Spencer Whittaker joined Burnley as Secretary/Manager in the 1903–04 season. He was successful in recruiting new players, including the likes of goalkeeper Jerry Dawson plus Dugald McFarlane and Billy Green. It was 16 April 1910 when tragedy struck, for some reason he fell from an overnight train just outside Crewe when going to London to register a player for that days league fixture at Turf Moor against Manchester City, and was immediately killed.

3. **C.**   In Burnley's qualifying third round tie at Keswick on 31 October 1903, they beat the home side 8–0 with William Jackson scoring four goals followed by David Walders with three. The other was scored by James Crawford. In the following round, Burnley lost at Darwen 0–3.

4 **C.**   Bury, who beat Burnley at Turf Moor in the first round of the FA Cup on 27 January 1900 were eventual winners of that competition beating Southampton 4–0 at Crystal Palace in the Final. Three season later, they won the FA Cup for a second time beating Derby County by a record 6–0 score line.

5 **A.**   Half-back Joe Taylor made his 300th league appearance against Leicester Fosse on 6 January 1906. He made a total of 323 League appearances for Burnley and a further 21 FA Cup appearances after joining from Bacup in 1893. He finally retired in May 1907.

6 **C.** Dick Smith who joined Burnley from Workington in September 1904 became the clubs record top league goalscorer in the 1907–08 season beating the current holder Jimmy Ross' 23 goals of ten seasons previously. Dick Smith was the previous seasons top League goalscorer with 16 and in his six seasons at Burnley made a total of 185 senior appearances scoring a total of 75 goals. He returned to Workington in July 1910.

7. **C.** If Burnley's FA Cup opponents of the 1900–01 season were to meet at the present time, they would be playing Manchester United and Birmingham City. Manchester United changed their name from Newton Heath at the beginning of the 1902–03 season. Birmingham City changed their name from Small Heath to Birmingham in 1905, City was added to the name in 1943.

8 **C.** Goalkeeper Jack Hillman final game for Burnley was at Walsall in the first round of the FA Cup on 25 January 1902 where they were beaten 0–1. He had a total of three spells at Burnley since joining in 1890, making a total of 188 senior appearances, including the game at Nottingham Forest on 28 April 1900 where he tried to bribe the Forest players to throw the game in order to avoid relegation for a second time.

9. **B.** Goalkeeper Jack Hillman joined Manchester City in January 1902 and went on to make a total of 116 senior appearances for them, which included being a member of the City side that beat Bolton Wanderers 1–0 in the 1904 FA Cup Final at Crystal Palace. He left Manchester City in 1906 and joined Southern League Millwall. He later returned to Burnley in a training capacity.

10 **C.** Although leading league goalscorer Cornelius Hogan was born in Malta, he was in fact English as his mother was there with his father who was doing military service. He was signed from Watford in November 1901 and made a total of 46 senior

appearances scoring 19 goals. He was leading League goalscorer in both the 1901–02 and 1902–03 season before being released in April 1903.

1. **C.** Dick Smith, Bert Freeman, and George Beel were all record league scoring Burnley players. Dick Smith was record leading goalscorer in the 1907–08 season with 24 goals scored. This was overtaken when Bert Freeman scored a total of 32 goals in the 1912–13 season. In the 1927–28 season, George Beel scored 35 times, which has remained a record feat since.

2. **B.** Tommy Boyle was Burnley's record £1,150 signing in September 1911 from Barnsley. He became club captain and lifted both the FA Cup in 1914 and Football League championship trophy in 1921. In his twelve years at the club, he made a total of 236 senior appearances scoring a total of 43 goals before moving to Wrexham in April 1923.

3. **A.** Burnley played a total of eight FA cup ties including the final, scoring a total of 13 goals. Two of these ties were goalless, against Sunderland and Sheffield United in the semi-final. They conceded just four goals in all eight ties.

4. **A.** The attendance at the Crystal Palace stadium for the FA Cup Final of 1914 between Burnley and Liverpool was 72,776 and would be the last time a Final would be played there since it first staged the event since 1895. Two lots of admission had to be paid, the first to get into the Exhibition grounds and the second to enter the Stadium.

5. **C.** A total of 22 goals were scored by Burnley in nine Football League cup ties in the 1982–83 season that got them to the Semi-Final where they were beaten by eventual winners Liverpool. They scored eight goals in the first two-legged ties against Bury. The biggest giant killing act came at Tottenham Hotspur on 19 January when Burnley beat the London side 4–1.

6. **B.** Thirteen clubs have beaten Burnley in the early rounds of the FA Cup including the Semi-finals and Final. They include. Notts County 1893–94. Sheffield United 1898–99. Bury. 1899–1900. Manchester United 1908–09. Bradford City 1910–11. Huddersfield Town 1921–22. Sheffield Wednesday 1934–35. Arsenal 1949–50. Aston Villa 1956–57. Tottenham Hotspur 1960–61 and 1961–62. West Ham United 1963–64 and Chelsea 1969–70.

7. **B.** Six clubs have beaten Burnley in the early rounds of the Football League Cup including the semi-finals and final. They include. Aston Villa 1960–61. Swindon Town 1968–69. Wolverhampton Wanderers 1979–80. Liverpool 1982–83 and 1994–95 and finally Manchester City 2019–20.

8. **A.** Three Burnley goalkeepers did in fact all play at the same time for their countries on 29 March 2022. They were Nick Pope for England versus Ivory Coast. Wayne Hennessy for Wales versus Czech Republic and Bailey Peacock Farrell for Northern Ireland versus Hungary. Bailey Peacock Farrell although loaned to Sheffield Wednesday is registered as a Burnley player.

9. **B.** It was nearly 14 years that Burnley failed to have player representing their country since Tommy Willighan was selected for Northern Ireland against Scotland at Hampden Park on 16 September 1933. Billy Morris for Wales was the next international player when selected against Northern Ireland in Belfast on 16 April 1947.

10. **A.** Of the 12 football clubs that joined the Football League in 1888, six of these were from the Midlands with four of them from Lancashire and two from east Lancashire. The east Lancashire teams were Burnley and Blackburn Rovers.

Quiz 38 Answers and Facts

1 **B.** Leading Premiership goalscorer Steven Fletcher scored a total of eight goals. He joined Burnley for a record £3 million fee in June 2009 and played just one season making a total of 35 senior appearances. He was transferred by Burnley to Wolverhampton Wanderers a season later for a record outgoing fee of £6.5 million. He represented Scotland a total of 33 times.

2. **A.** Paul Gascoigne made a total of three full appearances for Burnley when he was transferred to the club from Everton in March 2002. He also made three league appearances as a substitute and was unfortunate not to score. He was released from his contract a month later.

3. **B.** Frank Teasdale took over as chairman at Burnley in May 1985 from John E. Jackson. He stayed at Burnley till December 1998 when businessman Barry Kilby took over. Frank Teasdale saw some turbulent times whilst Chairman, which included the 1987 Orient game. He had some successes which included two promotions in 1992 and 1994 but the club were relegated the following season from the First Division back into the third tier of English football.

4. **A.** Bob Lord, undoubtedly Burnley's most colourful chairman died in 1981. The local Burnley businessman took over the chairmanship in June 1955 from William Hopkinson and was in the position until October 1981. He saw numerous successes at Burnley, including the League Championship of 1960 and two runners up successes in 1962 as well as European football. He also witnessed the bad times when they were relegated to the third tier of English football in 1980.

5. **C.** Goalkeeper Billy O'Rourke did in fact concede seven goals in his Burnley debut at Queens Park Rangers on 27 October 1979. He made a total of 17 senior appearances for Burnley over a six-year period before joining Chester City in March 1984.

6. **B.** When Burnley lost to Swindon Town 0–2 at Turf Moor on 10 January 1948, the visiting manager was ex-Burnley legend Louis Page, who made a total of 259 senior appearances and scored a total of 115 goals. His record of six goals scored at Birmingham in 1926 remains unbeaten to this day.

7. **A.** Frank Hill, Burnley's manager from September 1948 to May 1954 moved to Preston North End who were also a First Division club. He became Burnley's first ever Scottish manager and his best season was in the 1952–53 season when they were challenging for the league title having been top of the division a couple of times. They eventually finished in sixth place six points behind the leaders Wolverhampton Wanderers.

8. **B.** Tom Nicol was the first Burnley player to have scored a hat-trick on his League debut. It was in the First Division league game against Preston North End at Turf Moor on 7 March 1891 when he scored in the 7th, 40th and 80th minutes to seal a 6–2 victory for Burnley.

9. **C.** Claude Lambie became the first Burnley player to have scored two successive hat-tricks. The first was at Aston Villa on 8 November 1890 which resulted in a 4–4 draw. The second was seven days later against Derby County at Turf Moor and he also added a fourth to break two club records, being the first player to score four goals in a game for Burnley.

10. **A.** Tommy Cummings also left Burnley in March 1963 joining club legend Jimmy McIlroy who went to Stoke City. Tommy Cummings had made a total of 479 senior appearances since

he first joined them in October 1947. He joined Mansfield Town as Player Manager.

1. **C.** Both full-backs David Holt and Ian Wood were transferred from Oldham Athletic in July 1980 and May 1980. They both together made their debuts as full-backs against Newport County in the opening game at Turf Moor on 16 August 1980 and played together a total of nine times that season. Ian Wood was subsequently released from his contract in November 1981 and David Holt stayed longer having made a total of 110 senior appearances before retiring in 1983.

2. **A.** The Football authorities decided to change the points system from two points for a win to three points at the start of the 1981–82 football season. Burnley first gained three points in their second league game of the season beating Plymouth Argyle at Turf Moor 1–0 on 5 September 1981. Burnley that season won the Third Division title with 80 points compared to 61 with the old system that would have won the title by four clear points. They won the title with the new system on goal difference from second placed Carlisle United.

3. **B.** Non-league Runcorn held Burnley to a goalless draw in the first round FA Cup tie at Turf Moor on 21 November 1981. Burnley won the replay three days later at Runcorn 2–1 and eventually made it as far as the fourth round of the competition, losing at Shrewsbury Town 0–1 having also beaten another non-League club Altrincham at Turf Moor 6–1 in the previous round.

4 **A.** Tony Morley was transferred to Aston Villa for a record fee of £220,000 In June 1979. He joined Burnley from Preston North End in February 1976 and had a second spell at Burnley when he was loaned by West Bromwich Albion in October 1988. In total he made 89 full senior appearances plus 16 as a

substitute before moving back to West Bromwich Albion a month later.

5. **C.** Willie Irvine, who scored a record total of 37 goals in the 1965–66 season, also scored a total of four goals from five internationals for Northern Ireland in the same season. He scored a goal against Scotland on 2 October 1965 in Belfast, against England at Wembley on 10 November 1965, against Albania on 24 November 1965 in Tirana and against Wales in Cardiff on 30 March 1966.

6 **C.** Burnley, a Second Division side made it to the 1934-35 FA Cup semi-final against Sheffield Wednesday at Villa Park on 16 March 1935. They were outclassed by the First Division opponents losing the tie 0–3. On the way to the semi-finals, they beat Mansfield Town, Luton Town, Nottingham Forest after a replay and Birmingham City in the sixth round.

7. **B.** Jack Bruton, who joined Burnley in March 1925 from non-league Horwich RML made a total of 176 senior appearances scoring 44 goals up until his transfer to Blackburn Rovers in December 1929. Whilst at Burnley, he was selected for England for three internationals, against France, Belgium and Scotland, none of which were on home soil.

8. **C.** Adam Blacklaw reached a total of 172 consecutive League appearances at Elland Road against Leeds United on 15 March 1965. He conceded five goals and was subsequently replaced by Harry Thomson. The 172 consecutive run began at Blackpool on 23 March 1961 which ended as a goalless draw. He finally joined Blackburn Rovers in July 1967 having made a total of 383 senior appearances.

9. **A.** Ralph Coates was transferred to Tottenham Hotspur in May 1971 following Burnley's relegation from the First Division for a

fee of £190,000. In his eight years at Burnley, who he joined as an apprentice in June 1963, he made a total of 257 plus senior appearances scoring 32 goals in total. He was selected for England twice against Northern Ireland in April 1970 and against Greece as a substitute in April 1971 with both internationals played at Wembley.

10 **A.**   A new club crest was introduced for the 1978–79 season when invitations were made to the general public for a redesign. The club crest was used up until the Championship Play-off Final at Wembley in 2009 when Burnley beat Sheffield United 1–0 to be promoted back to the first tier of English football. The old crest was reintroduced at the beginning of the 2009–10 season to celebrate 50 years since becoming champions of England.

Quiz 40 Answers and Facts

1. **B.** Sheffield United were the first non-league club to have knocked Burnley out of the FA Cup on 18 January 1890. Sheffield United play on one of the oldest grounds in England Bramall Lane and have won the competition four times. They were former members of the newly formed Football League Second Division in 1892

2. **B.** Only two Burnley managers have been at the helm twice. The first was Harry Potts from January 1958 to February 1970 and February 1977 to October 1979. The second was Brian Miller from October 1979 to January 1983 and then from July 1986 to January 1989.

3. **A.** Only two Burnley players made league appearances in both the abandoned league game at Turf Moor on 26 August 1939 and the replayed fixture on 31 August 1946. The players were Arthur Woodruff who played as a half-back in the 1939 game and reverted to the right-back position in 1946 and half-back George Bray.

4. **C.** Charles Sutcliffe, Secretary at Burnley was installed as Club Chairman in May 1896, becoming the fifth to take up that post. It was thought that he was the first ever manager at the club but this was dispelled some years later with Harry Bradshaw becoming the first in the 1894–95 season.

5 **B.** Tom Morrison, Burnley's controversial winger was in fact the first club player to have played for Northern Ireland. His first selection was on 4 March 1899 in Belfast against Wales and a further three appearances followed against Wales for a second time and against Scotland and England. He made a further three selections whilst at Manchester United.

6. **B.**   Burnley's controversial goalkeeper Jack Hillman, who was found guilty of attempting to bribe the Nottingham Forest players at Trent Bridge on 28 April 1900 to ensure the club avoided relegation was sentenced to a one year ban as well as a large fine. In present day circumstances, to quote the Sheffield Wednesday incident of the 1960s he would have faced a jail sentence plus a ban for life. Jack Hillman returned to Burnley for the opening league game at Lincoln City on 7 September 1901.

7. **A.**   Burnley's team strip, before the introduction of the green and white one, was red shirts and white shorts. There have been many variations including the first light blue and white stripes followed by all blue shirts. Pink and white stripes. Amber and black stripes plus amber and claret stripes. The red and white kit had been around from 1896 to the beginning of the 1900–01 season when the green shirts were introduced.

8. **A.**   The first London league club that Burnley defeated were Woolwich Arsenal at Turf Moor on 1 December 1900 with the game finishing 3–0 to Burnley. Woolwich Arsenal, who had recently joined the Second Division of the Football League would eventually become one of English footballs biggest clubs having escaped liquidation a few years later. It was the sale of future Burnley legend Bert Freeman to Everton that saved the club.

9 **B.**   In the 1925–26 season when the rules of the offside system were changed, Burnley, not compliant with the change conceded over six goals in the following games. 0–10 at Aston Villa. 1–6 at Manchester United. 3–8 at Manchester City, 1–8 at Bury, 3–6 at Blackburn Rovers and 1–6 at Sheffield United .

10 **C.** The first Burnley Supporters Club was formed in 1932 following the poor league attendance of just 3,135 for a home fixture against Southampton on 2 January 1932. Attendances improved not long after, although the home attendances did not go above double of the previous seasons. In 1974, Burnley's travelling London supporters formed their own supporters club, aptly named the London Clarets which had the blessing from Burnley Chairman Bob Lord and has been going strong to the present day.

Quiz 41 Answers and Facts

1. **C.** Burnley had a total of 9 players that appeared in both the promotion seasons of 2013–14 and 2015–16 seasons. They were Goalkeeper, Tom Heaton. Full-backs, Michael Duff and Ben Mee. Half-backs, David Jones, Mike Kightly, Scott Arfield and Dean Marney. Forwards, Sam Vokes and Ashley Barnes.

2. **A.** The last time previous to the 2017–18 season that they failed to score from the penalty spot in all senior competitions was in the 1963–64 season, which amounted to 42 league games and five FA Cup ties. The next penalty to be scored was by Brian O'Neil in the fifth league game of the season against Everton at Turf Moor on 5 September 1964. The total number of games played without a penalty being scored was 52 games.

3. **C.** Graham Alexander scored a total of 11 goals from all senior games throughout the 2008–09 promotion winning season. The first was at Nottingham Forest on 13 September 2008 where he scored from the spot twice. His total from all the championship games played was nine and he scored at West Bromwich Albion in an FA Cup tie, as well as another at Reading in the play-off second leg Semi-final to make it a record total of 11 goals scored from the Burnley mid fielder

4. **B.** Throughout the Second World War, many local friendlies were played and many players were drawn from other clubs. Harry Holdcroft Preston North End's goalkeeper made a total of 27 appearances for Burnley in the 1941–42 season. He was the unfortunate incumbent who conceded a record 13 goals at Blackpool on 7 March 1942 and this was repeated two days later at Turf Moor where the Seasiders scored six. The Blackpool side boasted the likes of Stan Mortensen and Stanley Matthews in their side.

5. **A.** The 1987 Orient game hero Ian Britton came to Burnley from Blackpool in August 1986 and played in various positions throughout the 1986–87 campaign which totalled 37 league appearances. Up until the Orient game at Turf Moor on 9 May 1987, he had only scored two goals, but it was his third goal in the 48th minute that saved Burnley from certain relegation to non-league football for the first time. He was released from the club at the end of May 1989 having made a total of 121 plus senior appearances.

6. **B.** Their were 3 Burnley players that appeared in all the Clubs 42 League games in the promotion winning season of 1946–47. They were Goalkeeper, Jimmy Strong. Full-back, Harry Mather and Half-back and captain Alan Brown. The 3 players also appeared in all the clubs 9 FA Cup ties to bring the total appearances to 51 which also included the 1947 FA Cup Final against Charlton Athletic.

7. **C.** Gordon Harris was the first Burnley player to have scored in the Football League Cup. Burnley were drawn to play at Cardiff City in the second round of this first ever season of this competition on 24 October 1960. Winger Gordon Harris opened up the scoring in the 35th minute and added a further two goals with the result a 4–0 win for Burnley. They progressed to the semi-final of this competition only to be beaten by eventual winners Aston Villa. For the following five seasons, Burnley withdrew from this competition.

8. **B.** Just 1 Burnley player made all 22 league appearances in their very first season of 1888–89. He was half-back Danny Friel and he also appeared in both the clubs 2 FA Cup ties. He made just 5 league appearances the following season before joining local rivals Nelson in November 1889.

9. **A.** Burnley made their 2,000th top tier league game on 20 December 2009 at Wolverhampton Wanderers where they were defeated 0–2. Having made their first season back

amongst the elite of English football for the first time since 1976, following a promising start, they were once again relegated to the Championship.

10. **B.** The trophy that Burnley were presented with in the 2015–16 season was a replica that has been in use since the reconstruction of the four leagues in the 1992–93 season.

Quiz 42 Answers and Facts

1. **C.** Burnley have been automatically promoted eight times. (the promotion in 1898 was through the test match system) The first was in the 1912–13 season from Division Two. The second was in 1946–47 season from Division Two. The third was from Division Two in the 1972–73 season. The fourth was from Division Three in the 1981–82 season. The fifth was from the Fourth Division in 1991–92 season. The sixth was from Division Two (new) in the 1999–2000 season. The seventh was from the Championship in 2013–14 season and the eighth was from the Championship in the 2015–16 season.

2. **A.** Burnley have been promoted from the play-off system twice although they were promoted through the test match system in the 1897–98 season. The first play-off win was against Stockport County at Wembley on 29 May 1994 having beaten Plymouth Argyle 3–1 on aggregate in the semi-finals. The result was a 2-1 win for Burnley that promoted them to the second tier of English football, courtesy of goals from David Eyres and Gary Parkinson. The second was at Wembley against Sheffield United on 25 May 2009 in the Championship play-off Final where a Wade Elliott first half goal secured a promotion to the top tier of English football. Burnley beat Reading 3–0 on aggregate in the semi-finals to secure their place in the Final.

3. **C.** Burnley have never had three consecutive 0–0 drawn league games until the 2014–15 season when the first drawn 0–0 game was at Turf Moor on 20 August 2014 against Manchester United. This was followed on 13 September at Crystal Palace where a second 0–0 drawn game occurred. The third was at Turf Moor on 20 September 2014 when visitors Sunderland were held 0–0.

4. **B.** Three Burnley players appeared in all the 46 league games of the 2013–14 promotion winning season. They were Goalkeeper, Tom Heaton, Defender, Jason Shackell and Midfielder David Jones. Burnley goalkeeper Tom Heaton was however red carded at Brighton in his fourth appearance with Alex Cisak taking over for the remainder of the game.

5 **C.** The two other Premier League clubs that were relegated with Burnley in the 2009–10 season were bottom club Portsmouth with 19 points and second from bottom Hull City with 30 points. Burnley who were third bottom had also finished on 30 points.

6. **C.** Burnley lost eight consecutive League games from 2 January 1995 till 4 March 1995 when they finally drew 1–1 at home to West Bromwich Albion. The last time that occurred was in the 1889–90 season when Burnley lost eight consecutive games from 2 November 1889 to 1 March 1890.

7 **A.** No Burnley player made all 42 league appearances in the Fourth Division Championship winning season of 1991–92. The closest was Forward, John Deary and Half-back Stephen Davis who both made 40 appearances each.

8. **C.** Andy Lochhead was the first Burnley player to have scored five in the FA Cup at Turf Moor in a third-round replay against Bournemouth and Boscombe Athletic on 25 January 1966. He has also scored five goals in a League match at Turf Moor against Chelsea on 25 April 1965 and is the only Burnley player to score five twice in all senior competitions

9. **C.** Bryan Flynn made a total of 34 appearances for Wales whilst at Burnley, from his first against Luxembourg as a substitute on 20 November 1974. Before his transfer to Leeds United, he made 21 international appearances He returned to Burnley in

1982 and made a further 13 international appearances, his last being against Israel in Tel Aviv on 10 June 1984. In all he made a total of 66 International appearances for Wales.

10 **B.** The first player to have scored in seven consecutive games was Willie Irvine when he scored his first at Leeds United on 30 October 1965. He scored in the following games against West Ham United, twice, Sunderland, Aston Villa, Liverpool, Tottenham Hotspur and finally with a hat-trick at Fulham, to record 10 goals scored from seven League games.

Quiz 43 Answers and Facts

1. **A.**   Burnley began the 1979–80 season without a win in their first 16 games. It put them bottom of the Second Division with seven points before their first win at home to Cambridge United on 24 November 1979. It was the worst start ever for Burnley in any season and it eventually relegated them for the first time to the third tier of English football.

2. **C.**   Defender Michael Duff who came to Burnley in July 2004 from Cheltenham Town where he had made over 300 appearances. He made a total of 383 senior appearances up until his last game at Charlton Athletic in May 2016. His debut for Burnley was on 7 August 2004 at Turf Moor against Sheffield United in a Championship fixture. He was also selected for Northern Ireland 21 times whilst a player at Burnley before he moved into management with his first club Cheltenham Town. He successfully managed them to promotion in the 2020–21 season. He is currently the manager at League One side Barnsley.

3. **A.**   When Jimmy Adamson retired from playing football in 1964 , he was approached by Sunderland but instead took over as assistant to Harry Potts. He had originally been coach for the England 1962 World Cup squad and turned down the full-time managers job prior to Alf Ramsey taking over. In February 1970, he replaced Harry Potts as Burnley manager and was in that position until he resigned in January 1976 to take over the managerial position at Sparta Rotterdam before joining Sunderland in the November of 1976. After two years at Sunderland, he joined Leeds United for a further two years before quitting football for good owing to the hostility he received from the Leeds United fan base.

4. **C.** When Burnley qualified for the Inter-Cities Fairs Cup competition, having finished third in the first division of 1962-63 season, it was deemed inappropriate for them to compete in this competition as Burnley was a Town and not a City. The rules of the competition were later changed which allowed them to enter the competition again in 1966 having once again finishing in third place in the first division of the Football League.

5. **A.** When Burnley legend Tommy Boyle left Burnley in April 1923. he joined Third Division North side Wrexham who had in the past few years joined the new set up. In the first season he was there, he made just seven appearances with the side finishing the season in 16th place in the division of the 1923–24 season. They were that season's Welsh Cup winners beating Merthyr Town 1–0 in the Final.

6. **C.** Burnley League Champions of the Football League in the 1920–21 season were beaten in the third round of the FA Cup by Second Division Hull City 0–3 having beaten Leicester City and Queens Park Rangers in the previous rounds. It was a time when they had prior to that tie gone 24 League games without defeat and would eventually reach 30 which would become a Division One record.

7. **B.** Max Seeburg was the first foreign player to have played for Burnley. He made his league debut against Lincoln City in the opening League game against Lincoln City as centre-forward on 3 September 1910.

The German player was signed from London amateur side Leyton and made a total of 18 senior appearances before joining Grimsby Town a year later.

.

8. **A.** Jimmy McIlroy has been Burnley's top league goalscorer when he achieved this two seasons running in the 1956–57 season when he scored 13 and in the 1957–58 season when he scored 16. In his Burnley career of thirteen years, he scored a total of 131 goals from 497 senior appearances.

9. **B.** Jimmy McIlroys final League game for Burnley was at Turf Moor on 29 December 1962 where they beat Sheffield Wednesday 4–0. For two solid months, no League football was played owing to one of the worst ever winters on record. Finances were tight and it was seen by Bob Lord and his associates that the only answer would be to sell their main asset to Stoke City for £25,000 to ease the financial problem that had risen . His final appearance for Burnley was at Anfield against Liverpool in the FA Cup fourth round replay on 20 February 1963 where Burnley were beaten 1–2.

10 **B.** The only other known football club to share the title The Clarets are Essex non-league side Chelmsford City who have for the past few seasons played in the National League South. They have been established since 1878, four seasons before Burnley were founded as an Association Football Club.

Quiz 44 Answers and Facts

1. **C.** The Burnley Youth side won the FA Youth Cup in the 1967–68 season, beating Coventry City Youth 3–2 on aggregate in a two-legged Final. On the way to the Final they beat youth teams from Yorkshire AMS, Manchester City, Manchester United, Sheffield United and Everton in the two-legged Semi-final 3–2 on aggregate.

2. **A.** Burnley who were drawn to play Chelsea in the fourth round of the FA Cup scored a total of four goals from five ties. The first was at Turf Moor on 28 January 1956 which ended 1–1, with the replay at Stamford Bridge four evenings later again resulting 1–1 after extra-time. The third tie at St Andrews was again a 2–2 draw after extra-time five evening later. The fourth, at Highbury, after extra time was 0–0 a week later with the fifth at White Hart Lane on 15 February 1956 which ended 2–0 to Chelsea. A total of 540 minutes of football was played by both sides.

3. **B.** William Tait was the first ever Burnley player to score at West Bromwich Albion on 29 September 1888, long before the club played at the Hawthorns. The result was a 3–4 defeat for Burnley in which was their fourth away fixture in the inaugural Football League season. All the first four fixtures were played at away opposition with Willian Tait's scoring from four games standing at four goals scored. He played his final league game for Burnley in their first league game at Turf Moor, which was his fifth appearance, scoring in the 60th minute against Bolton Wanderers to bring his total goal scoring to five. He was for some reason released from the club in October 1888.

4. **A.** Willie Irvine holds the post war scoring record of 29 goals from the 1965–66 season. He scored a total of three hat-tricks against Northampton Town, Fulham and Nottingham Forest and also became the first in that season to score in seven consecutive League games. In total he also scored five in the FA Cup, three in the League Cup to bring his total to 37, although he shares this feat with Jimmy Robson who scored an overall total of 34 from all three domestic competitions plus three goals he scored in the European Cup competition.

5. **B.** The first League season that Burnley conceded over 100 goals was in the 1925–26 season where they conceded 108 goals. The new offside ruling caught them out and in six League games they conceded six or more goals. The highest that season was at Villa Park against Aston Villa on the opening day when the result to Villa was 0–10. A 3–8 score at Manchester City and 1–8 defeat at Bury brought the total conceded to 61 from 20 League games. On the plus side. Burnley scored a total of 85 goals which included Louis Page's six goals at Birmingham that avoided relegation by one point to send Manchester City down (the club that beat them 3–8).

6. **C.** Eddie Howe, who joined Burnley as manager from AFC Bournemouth in January 2011 replacing Brian Laws, was in charge of his first Championship game at Scunthorpe United on 22 January 2011 which ended 0–0. Burnley finished the season in eleventh position and in the following 2011–12 season finished thirteenth. In October 2012, he resigned from his position stating domestic reasons and returned to AFC. Bournemouth where he successfully won the Championship in the 2014–15 season. He is currently manager at Newcastle United.

7. **B.** When Burnley lost to Charlton Athletic in the 1947 FA Cup Final, they had seven Second Division league fixtures to fulfil. In the May of 1947, they beat Newport County 3–0 and lost both to Manchester City and Fulham 0–1. They beat Leicester City 4–1 and drew 1–1 with Bury. They clinched promotion to the First Division having beaten West Ham United at Upton Park 5–0 and finally drew 1–1 at Millwall in which was Burnleys first ever league fixture in the month of June.

8 **B.** When the rules were changed to allow promotion and relegation from the Football League and the newly formed non-league division, The bottom club in the Football League would be relegated allowing the top non-league club to replace them. Scarborough were the first team to have won promotion under these new terms and it was Lincoln City who were relegated with Burnley, having survived by just one point to finish in 22nd place. In the following 1987–88 season, Burnley were beaten by Scarborough in both home and away fixtures 0–1.

9. **B.** The only Burnley player to have made all 46 league appearances in the 1999–2000 season was goalkeeper Paul Crichton who also made all the club's League Cup and FA Cup ties(6 in total) plus the Clubs 1 Football League trophy tie against Wigan Athletic to total 53 appearances for the season.

10. **B.** There were a total of 14 Burnley players who have represented England prior to World War Two. They are; Billy Bannister with one cap, Tommy Boyle, one cap, Jack Bruton three caps, James Crabtree three caps, Jerry Dawson two caps, Bert Freeman three caps, Jack Hill eight caps, Jack Hillman one cap, Bob Kelly 11 caps, Eddie Mosscrop two caps, Louis Page seven caps, George Waterfield one cap, Billy Watson three caps and Jack Yates one cap.

Quiz 45 Answers and Facts

1. **A.** A total of six Burnley players made all 42 Second Division appearances that season. They were, goalkeeper Alan Stevenson, full-back Keith Newton, half-backs Colin Waldron and Jim Thompson, forwards Frank Casper and Leighton James.

2. **C.** Dave Thomas was sold to Queens Park Rangers having made 11 League appearances for Burnley. He was sold for a record fee £165,000 from the London side. He had been at Burnley since October 1967 as an apprentice and had made a total of 175 plus appearances scoring a total of 23 goals. He would eventually join Everton, having made 182 senior appearances for Rangers and made a total of 71 senior appearances for the Merseysiders. He also made eight international appearances for England.

3. **B.** Just two players made their Burnley debuts that season, with Keith Newton and Ray Hankin coming late in the season. Keith Newton was purchased from Everton in June 1972 and made his debut for Burnley in the opening league game at Turf Moor on 12 August 1972 against Carlisle United. He would make a total of 253 senior appearances for Burnley before being released from his contract in May 1978. Ray Hankin was also an apprentice and came on as a substitute for Paul Fletcher in the last but one game at Turf Moor against Luton Town. He would make a total of 137 plus senior appearances before being transferred to Leeds United in September 1976.

4. **B.** In the Charity Shield Final at Main Road between Manchester City and Burnley on 18 August 1973 just a single goal settled result, the goal was scored by half-back Colin Waldron. It was the first time that the Shield had been won outright by

Burnley, having shared the spoils against Wolverhampton Wanderers in 1961 and losing to Tottenham Hotspur in 1921. Colin Waldron, who was purchased from Chelsea in October 1967 would spend nine years at Burnley making a total of 356 senior appearances before moving to Manchester United in June 1976. He would join the list of 20 Burnley players who have made over 300 senior appearances for the club.

5. **B.** Paul Fletcher was the leading League goalscorer that season with 15 goals. He scored a hat-trick at Turf Moor on 21 October against Cardiff City in Burnley's 3–0 win. He would repeat his performance a season later in the First Division when he was leading league goalscorer with 13 goals. Paul Fletcher was purchased by Burnley from Bolton Wanderers in March 1971 and in his nine years at the club make a total of 349 plus senior appearances, scoring 86 goals before moving to Blackpool in February 1980.

6. **B.** The last time that Burnley were Second Division champions was in the 1897–98 season when they won the division having been relegated the previous. They had to qualify for promotion through the Test Match System that was finally abandoned, owing to it being abused, with both Burnley and Stoke City playing out a goalless draw which enabled both clubs to qualify for promotion. Burnley who played 30 league games that season lost just two with goalscoring legend Jimmy Ross scoring a club record 23 goals.

7 **A.** Burnley lost just four league games in the 1972–73 season. The first was at Orient on 11 November 1972 losing 1–2. The second was at Queens Park Rangers ,who would be eventual league runners up losing 0–2 on 27 January 1973. The third loss was at Turf Moor on 10 March 1973 against Sheffield Wednesday who beat them 1–0 and the fourth game was

against Nottingham Forest who beat them 3–0 at Trent Bridge on 31 March 1973.

8. **B.** Burnley in the first 16 league fixtures of the 1972–73 season, were unbeaten. In those 16 unbeaten games, Burnley drew nine of them and were top of the division with 23 points. In game number 17, they were beaten 1–2 by Orient at Turf Moor on 11 November 1972. Burnley remained top of the division for most of the remaining season with the main threat being posed by runners up Queens Park Rangers .

9. **C.** John Angus who made 520 senior appearances for Burnley from becoming a junior to being one of the longest serving players to have appeared for the club. He retired from playing at the end of the 1971–72 season and a well-deserved testimonial was arranged. having been with the club for over 15 years. The testimonial was arranged at Turf Moor with an attendance of 16,000, 2,000 more than attended the home matches throughout the season. An Old Stars team played a Young Clarets side which was a credit to John Angus who had been an excellent servant to Burnley Football Club.

10 **A.** Leighton James made a total of six international appearances for Wales in the promotion season of 1972–73. He was capped against England, three times , Poland, Scotland and Northern Ireland. He scored for Wales against Poland at Ninian Park, Cardiff on 28 March 1972 and at the end of that season had made a total of nine international appearances to date for Wales whilst at Burnley.

Quiz 46 Answers and Facts

1 **C.** Burnley goalkeeper Tom Heaton came to Burnley at the beginning of the 2013–14 season from Bristol City. He started his footballing career at Manchester United but unable to make any appearances, was loaned to Swindon Town, Royal Antwerp, Cardiff City, Queens Park Rangers, Rochdale and Wycombe Wanderers making a total of 63 senior appearances for all six clubs. He made a permanent move to Cardiff City before being transferred to Bristol City. He joined Burnley for the beginning of the 2013–14 season and was involved in two promotions, as well as later earning an England cap.

2. **B.** In the 2013–14 promotion season, goalkeeper Tom Heaton conceded just 36 goals in 46 League games It was the best performance since Alan Stevenson's 35 goals conceded in the 1972–73 season and the third best post war performance. with Jimmy Strong's 29 goals in the 1946–47 season the best of all time.

3. **A.** Alex Cisak was Tom Heaton replacement in the 58th minute, owing to Tom Heaton being sent off for handling the ball outside his area at Brighton and Hove Albion on 24 August 2013. The score at the time was 1–0 to Brighton who added a further goal to make the result 2–0 to the home side.

4. **B.** Midfielder Scott Arfield made his League debut for Burnley on 3 August 2013 at Turf Moor against Bolton Wanderers when he replaced Junior Stanislas in the 37th minute. He was signed from Huddersfield Town and made a further seven league appearances to the end of his first season at Burnley. The following season he became a Premier League player but the club were unfortunately relegated that season. A season later,

Burnley were Championship winners with Scott being part of the team. He had the honour also of representing Canada 29 times. He made a total of 193 senior appearances for Burnley as well as scoring 22 goals before his move to Rangers at the end of the 2017–18 season.

5. **B.** Danny Ings scored at total of 21 League goals in the 2013–14 season from 40 appearances. His first was at Sheffield Wednesday on 10 August 2013. He also scored one FA Cup goal and three Football League Cup goals to bring his overall record to 25 for the season. He scored a total of four braces.

6. **C.** Jimmy Strong conceded a total of 29 goals from 42 League games which was a club record. He also conceded just three goals from Burnley's FA Cup run of nine Cup Ties. He broke the club record for the most Football League games having not conceded a goal. He didn't concede a goal for a total of 675 minutes.

7 **B.** The first foreign player to have played for Burnley was German born Max Seeburg who made his league debut as a centre-forward at Turf Moor against Lincoln City on 3 September 1910. He was signed from London amateur side Leyton and made a total of 18 senior appearances before moving to Grimsby Town a season later .

8. **B.** Thomas Midgley was the only player to have played both Rugby football and League football for Burnley. He made many friendly appearances before Burnley became members of the Football League in 1888. He made his one and only league game at Stoke in the 1888-89 season.

9. **A.** Goalkeeper Adam Blacklaw made a total of 60 senior appearances for Burnley in the 1960–61 season. He made 41 League appearances, 7 FA Cup appearances. 7 Football League

appearances. 4 European Cup appearances and 1 Charity shield appearance, a club record.

10 **B.** Burnley having beaten Aston Villa 3–2 in the third round of the FA Cup and Bury 4–1 in the fourth were drawn to play Arsenal in the fifth round at Turf Moor on 20 February 1937. The result was 1–7 thrashing from the league champions of England.

Quiz 47 Answers and Facts

1. **B.**   Goalkeeper Jerry Dawson in fact made 568 senior appearances for Burnley. He made 522 League appearances 45 FA Cup appearances and one Charity Shield appearance totalling 568 not 569. There was a dispute in the original figures as he actually played 45 FA Cup appearances not 46. Jerry Dawson had been absent from 1 March 1923 and resumed playing on 23 March with stand-in goalkeeper Sammy Page taking his position and was credited with one of the FA Cup ties against Fulham instead of Jerry Dawson.

2. **A.**   The first Burnley manager to have won promotion twice was Jimmy Mullen. The first time was the Fourth Division Championship in the 1991–92 season having been appointed in the October of 1991. Two seasons later, he took them to Wembley for the Division Two Play-off Final against Stockport County with the result 2–1 to Burnley to secure First Division football for the club.

3. **C.**   Burnley's first ever London opponents were London Scottish who met Burnley at Turf Moor on New Year's Day 1884 with the result 2–2 and it apparently attracted a large crowd for a game that was said to be very interesting.

4. **A.**   Burnley's striker Andre Gray scored a total of 25 league goals in the 2015–16 Championship winning season but did not score in any of the other Cup competitions. He scored a hat-trick for Burnley on 28 December 2015 at Turf Moor against Bristol City which become a revival for the club which had a 23 League game unbeaten run.

5. **C.**   In the first season that Burnley participated in the Football League season of 1888–89, nine of the recorded home game

attendances averaged a total of 4,454. The highest attendance was against Preston North End at Turf Moor on 15 December 1888 ,the eventual champions with the result 2–2.

6. **A.** Bert Freeman was the second highest League hat-trick scorer, second to George Beel. His first was at Fulham on 28 October 1911 and was followed by a second two months later against Glossop. He scored a third in the return match at Turf Moor against Fulham. In the 1912–13 season, he scored his fourth against Leicester Fosse and completed his fifth in the first division home game against Derby County on 11 April 1914, two weeks before scoring the winning goal in the Cup Final of 1914 against Liverpool.

7. **A.** Only one Burnley player has ever scored a hat-trick for England, which was Jack Yates on 2 March 1889 against Ireland at Anfield, then the home of Everton FC. The final result was 6–1 to England and for some apparent reason was never selected again. The closest to come to a hat–trick was Bob Kelly and Billy Elliott who both scored two goals apiece.

8. **C.** Burnley legend Jimmy McIlroy scored a total of 10 goals from 51 Internationals for Northern Ireland whilst at Burnley. His first was in his 16th appearance against England in Belfast on 6 October 1956 which ended 1–1. His 10th and final goal for Northern Ireland was at Wembley on 22 November 1961 against England which once again ended 1–1.

9. **B.** Burnley goalkeeper Alan Stevenson made the second most senior appearances for the club which included 438 league appearances, 33 FA Cup appearances, 36 League Cup appearances, 19 Anglo Scottish Cup appearances, 7 Texaco Cup appearances, 4 Football League trophy appearances, 2 Watney Cup appearances and 1 Charity Shield appearance.

10. **A.** Ray Pointer holds the record for scoring the second highest amount of goals from all senior appearances. He has scored 118 League goals, 12 FA Cup goals, 2 League Cup goals, to bring his total to 132 scored. In third place on 131 was Jimmy McIlroy.

Quiz 48 Answers and Facts

1. **B.** It was the Second Division winning season of where they recorded 62 points, the highest that Burnley ever made under the old two points for a win system. They won 24. drew 14 and lost 4. The previous closest was in the 1960–61 Championship winning season with 59 points.

2. **A.** As of 30 June 2022, Burnley have had a total of 29 full-time Manager since the first Harry Bradshaw in August 1894. The longest serving three were John Haworth with over 14 years' service, Harry Potts with over 13 years' service in two spells at the club and Sean Dyche with over nine years' of service. Vincent Kompany was installed as Burnley manager in June 2022, being the 29th at the club.

3. **C.** Burnley signed both James Tarkowski and Andre Gray from Brentford. Andre Gray was the first in August 2015 and spent two seasons at the club before moving to Watford in August 2017. He made a total of 73 senior appearances scoring 32 goals. James Tarkowski was purchased in February 2016 and was sold to Everton in July 2022. He made 219 senior appearances and was capped for England twice.

4. **A.** Just 1 Burnley player half-back Joe Taylor made all 30 League appearances in the Second Division winning season of 1897–98 . He also made all 3 FA Cup appearances that season plus all 4 test matches to total 37 for the season. In his 14 years at the club, he made a then record 352 senior appearances before retiring in 1907.

5. **A.** The first ever abandoned league games between Burnley and Blackburn Rovers was on 12 December 1891, when the game at Turf Moor was played in atrocious conditions. When the

teams came out for the second half with Burnley 3–0 ahead, only a handful of Rovers players came out, with only goalkeeper Herbie Arthur left playing. The game was abandoned with the score remaining as it was and a penalty match was played later in March 1992 with the score 1–1.

6. **B.** The first ever abandoned game through floodlight failure was at Turf Moor on 17 December 1996 against Walsall in a FA Cup second round replay .The result at 45 minutes was 1–0 to Walsall. The game was eventually replayed six evenings later with Burnley winning the tie 4–2 on penalties with the score at 1–1 after 120 minutes.

7 **A.** Blackburn Olympic, who were a prominent side having been FA Cup winners, sent their A side to Turf Moor on 3 March 1883 in what was Burnley's third home game having lost the previous two to Rawtenstall 3–6 and Padiham 0–6, but it was third time lucky beating Olympic A 4–2 with Jonathan Wilkinson scoring twice and George Avery scoring the others and were probably the first ever recorded goalscorers at Turf Moor.

8. **C.** Jerry Dawson had just turned 34 when he was selected for England against Scotland at Villa Park on 8 April 1922 with the result a 0–1 defeat to England. It was his second England cap when six month previous he played in Belfast against Ireland with the result 1–1.

9 **A.** Only one player made his debut for Burnley in the 1961–62 season, Peter Simpson made his League debut for Burnley at Sheffield Wednesday on 30 April 1962 which ended in a heavy 0–4 defeat for Burnley. He replaced Jimmy McIlroy in that last League game of the season. The inside forward made two league appearances the following campaign before moving to Bury in August 1963.

10. **C.** Burnley on 16 September 1961 played Birmingham City at St Andrews and beat them 6–2 with Ray Pointer scoring a hat-trick. Four days later at Leicester City, they once again repeated that 6–2 result with both John Connelly and Jimmy Robson scoring two goals apiece.

Quiz 49 Answers and Facts

1. **A.** Keith Treacy was the first Burnley player to have been selected for The Republic of Ireland in the 2010–11 season. He played against Uruguay in Belfast as a substitute on 29 March 2011. He made further appearances that season against Northern Ireland, Scotland and Italy.

2. **B.** Burnley goalkeeper Brian Jensen was named the beast after a stuntman called Bryan Jensen flew a plane called the beast which when performing a stunt in America sadly killed him. Burnley's goalkeeper Brian Jensen was forever labelled the beast from then on.

3. **B.** Seven Burnley goalscorers have scored 25 or more league goals since the end of World War Two. They are; Peter McKay, 25,. 1955–56, Ray Pointer, 27, 1958–59 and 25, 1961–62, Jimmy Robson, 25, 1960–61, Willie Irvine, 29, 1965–66, Andy Payton, 27, 1999–2000, Charlie Austin, 25, 2012–13 and Andre Gray, 25, 2015–16.

4. **A.** There have been eight Burnley leading league goalscorers who have scored single figures Since World War Two. They are; Eric Probert, 5, 1970–71, Billy Hamilton, 7, 1979–80, Ron Futcher, 7, 1989–90, Winston White, 7, 1989–90, David Eyres, 8, 1994–95, Andy Payton, 9, 2000–01, Steven Fletcher, 8, 2009–10 and Maxwel Cornet, 9, 2021–22.

5 **C.** Burnley, who had been promoted through the Play-offs in the 2008–09 season signed up with Samuel Cooke and Company for the following Premiership season . The new team strip to mark the 50th anniversary of winning the League Championship was the old one with the V-neck and hooped

stockings. Cooke's had the deal for that one season only which ended with the club being relegated.

6. **B.** Wade Elliott was, for the second time, at the end of the 2007–08 season voted by the Burnley supporters as their player of the year. He will long be remembered for his goal for Burnley at Wembley against Sheffield United which won them promotion to the Premiership.

7. **B.** Peter Noble, who had made over 300 senior appearances for Burnley in over six seasons at the club, was responsible for knocking them out of the League Cup whilst playing for Swindon Town in the replayed semi-final tie at The Hawthorns on 18 December 1969. He scored the vital goal that took Swindon to Wembley, beating Burnley 3–2. Swindon won their first ever senior competition beating Arsenal in the Final.

8. **C.** On 24 August 1991, Burnley met Aldershot at Turf Moor beating them 2–0. The return match at Aldershot on 21 December 1991 was also a 2–1 victory for Burnley. Aldershot, because of financial difficulties, decided to resign from the Football League, all records were expunged. With six vital points lost, Burnley still had 6 points in hand to play and beat runners up Rotherham United to the Fourth Division Championship title.

9. **A.** Former Burnley player Paul Fletcher was awarded an MBE for services to football in 2007, having been involved as a designer of many football stadiums which included Wembley and he also a CEO at Burnley Football Club. He was also involved in the creation the University Campus of Football Business that had their headquarters at Turf Moor before it moved to Manchester City's stadium.

10. **A.** Fred Barron, prior to 1911, made the most appearances for Burnley including 400 league appearances and 23 FA Cup appearances to total 423 from 1898 to 1911

Quiz 50 Answers and Facts

1. **A.**   There have been 35 league games played on Christmas Day at Turf Moor. The last was on Christmas Day 1957 against Manchester City which ended 2–1 to Burnley. The first one was in 1993 against Sheffield United and there have been regular local derbies against Blackpool from 1905 to 1912. The biggest win was against Sheffield United in 1920 with Joe Anderson scoring four goals in the clubs 6–0 win. The biggest defeat was in 1924 when Huddersfield Town beat Burnley 1–5.

2. **B.**   Goalkeeper Gabor Kiraly, who joined Burnley in May 2007 and made a total of 27 senior appearances, left Burnley in June 2009 and did not represent his country whilst at the club. He made a total of 108 International Appearances for Hungary in total before retiring in May 2019. He was the most capped Burnley player ever.

3. **B.**   Burnley have conceded a total of three seven goal defeats at Turf Moor since they were first members in 1888. The first was on 3 November 1888 when they were beaten 1–7 by Blackburn Rovers. The second occasion was on 5 April 2003 against Watford when Burnley were beaten 4–7. In the same month of April, three weeks later, on the 26th, they lost 2–7 to Sheffield Wednesday.

4. **B.**   Burnley have conceded 10 goals in a League game twice. The first was the opening fixture at Aston Villa on 29 August 1925 where they were beaten 0–10. It was the season that the offside law of the game was changed and Burnley fell foul to this change, conceding a total of 108 goals that 1925–26 season. Three seasons later on 19 January 1929, Burnley were

beaten 0–10 at Bramall Lane to Sheffield United which became the second occurrence that the club conceded 10 goals.

5. **C.** Burnley have won the Lancashire Senior cup 12 times, the first when they defeated Blackburn Rovers at Accrington in the 1890 final 2–0. The next time was in 1915 when they beat Rochdale 4–1. The 12th and last time they have won the trophy was in 1993 when they beat Bury 4–3 on penalties after the clubs drew 2–2 at Turf Moor.

6 **B.** The late Burnley physiotherapist Jimmy Holland who was at the club for over 33 years. In all probability he was the longest serving member of staff followed By Bob Lord and Charlie Bates. A testimonial was arranged for him at Turf Moor on 8 August 1993 against Oldham Athletic and he passed away not long after.

7.**A.** Charles Massey was a brewery owner and was on the committee of the Burnley Rovers Rugby Club that proposed the transformation to Association Football from Rugby. The meeting of 18 May 1882 also proposed the name change by dropping the Rovers from the team name to just Burnley Football Club.

8 **C.** Scott Twine, before his move to Burnley in June 2022, played a total of 45 senior games for his previous club Milton Keynes Dons and scored a total of 20 goals. He was previously at Swindon Town and was loaned to Chippenham Town, Waterford and Newport County.

9. **A.** Manager Vincent Kompany, made a total of 265 senior appearances for Manchester City from 2008 to 2019. He won many honours with the club which included all three domestic trophies and was club captain for most of them. He was also selected for Belgium 85 times. He joined Anderlecht in 2020 as

player-manager before accepting the post of manager at Burnley in June 2022.

10 **B.** Burnley in the 1973–74 First Division season, remained unbeaten in the first seven fixtures before being defeated at Ipswich Town on 22 September 1973, 2–3. The only player at that time to make his debut was Peter Noble who replaced Mike Docherty. It was to be the most memorable season with Burnley finishing in sixth place in the division. The side included players from the previous campaign which included goalkeeper Alan Stevenson, half-backs Keith Newton, Martin Dobson and Colin Waldron. Forwards that remained were Jim Thomson, Doug Collins, Leighton James, Geoff Nulty and leading league goalscorer for the second consecutive season Paul Fletcher.

Thank you to the following.

Colin Waldron for his foreword for the book and Burnley Club team mate Paul Fletcher MBE for his support.

Don Hale in producing this publication.

Paul Dalling for his proofreading.

Wallace Chadwick and Ray Simpson for use of photographic materials.

Burnley Head of Business Partnerships, Carl Sanderson for his ongoing support.

Phil Whalley and the London Clarets for their continuous backing.

A big thank you to long time clarets supporter Brian Speak as always for use of recent photographic materials.

Dr Steve Green for his work on putting this publication together.

Other thank yous to the following who have given their support in the past.

Nick Wooster, Don Lennon, Damien Dewhurst and Paul Prosser.

And finally to my partner Eunice, who I love dearly, who has put up with me in getting all this together.

Printed in Great Britain
by Amazon